All About Faith 1

All About Faith

Book One
Jesus and the New Testament

Anne Boyle and Niall Boyle

Gill & Macmillan

Gill & Macmillan Ltd
Hume Avenue, Park West
Dublin 12
with associated companies throughout the world
www.gillmacmillan.ie

© Anne Boyle and Niall Boyle 2000
0 7171 2972 1

Print origination in Ireland by
Niamh Lehane Design Consultant

Imprimatur: Most Rev. Michael Smith, D.C.L., Bishop of Meath

The paper used in this book is made from the wood pulp of managed forests. For every tree felled, at least one tree is planted, thereby renewing natural resources.

All rights reserved.
No part of this publication may be copied, reproduced or transmitted in any form or by any means without written permission of the publishers or else under the terms of any licence permitting limited copying issued by the Irish Copyright Licensing Agency, The Writers' Centre, Parnell Square, Dublin 1.

Contents

1	Introduction to religion	1
2	The Sources	8
3	The Gospels I	10
4	The Gospels II	15
5	The setting	22
6	The Chosen People I	25
7	The Chosen People II	31
8	Awaiting the Messiah	36
9	The birth of Jesus	39
10	A portrait of Jesus	45
11	Life in Palestine	50
12	Growing up in Nazareth	55
13	Under Roman rule	59
14	John the Baptist	65
15	The baptism of Jesus	68
16	The temptations in the desert	70
17	Jesus begins His public ministry	72
18	The disciples	74
19	The Kingdom of God	77
20	The miracles of Jesus	81
21	Interpreting the miracles	85
22	Teaching by parables	89
23	Interpreting the parables	92
24	Jesus' entry into Jerusalem	96
25	Jesus in the temple	102
26	The Last Supper	108
27	The arrest and interrogation	111
28	The trial of Jesus	116
29	The crucifixion and death of Jesus	120
30	The burial of Jesus	124
31	The resurrection	127
32	Questions about the resurrection	131
33	The birth of Christianity	136
34	The expansion of Christianity	140
35	The titles of Jesus	145

CHAPTER ONE

INTRODUCTION TO RELIGION

Religion

It is difficult to find a single definition which adequately describes the various religions of the world. The following, however, can be offered as a guide:
Religion is a set of beliefs that usually involves the worship of a God or several gods.

Belief

All religions have beliefs but not all beliefs are religious. For example:
- God created the universe. = *Religious belief.*
- Leonardo da Vinci was the greatest artist who ever lived. = *Non-religious belief.*

To believe something means to accept that it is *true*. A person may have good reasons for believing it, but he/she cannot be absolutely certain that it is true. To believe something involves putting your trust or having *faith* in it. For example:
- The earth orbits the sun. = *Proven fact.*
- When you share a secret with a friend you are trusting him/her not to reveal it to anyone else without your permission. = *Act of faith.*

Religious belief involves a person putting his/her *faith* in a particular set of ideas about God and the meaning of life. An *organised* religion, such as Christianity, is where those people who share these beliefs gather together to *worship* God, i.e. show that God is *the* most important thing in their lives and that they wish to live *good* lives.

Catholic congregation worshipping at mass.

All About Faith

THE MAJOR WORLD RELIGIONS

NAME	FOUNDING DATE	PLACE (MODERN NAME)	FOUNDER	ESTIMATED N0. OF MEMBERS
Hinduism	3000-2500 B.C.	India	Unknown 'Rishis' i.e. wise men	c.750 million
Judaism	1700 B.C.	Iraq	Abraham	c.18 million
Buddhism	560 B.C.	India	Gautama (The Buddha)	c.320 million
Christianity	5 B.C.	Israel	Jesus Christ	c.2,000 million
Islam	A.D. 570	Saudi Arabia	Mohammed	c.1,300 million
Sikhism	A.D. 1499	Pakistan	Nanak	c.18 million

Signs and Symbols

Each one of the major world religions has its own distinctive set of beliefs and *rituals* (i.e. *forms of worship where its members gather to celebrate their faith in God*). Each religion expresses its particular identity through the use of *signs* and *symbols*.

In prayers people use sounds — words — to communicate particular ideas about God.

In a similar way, the members of a religion use *visual images* (e.g. the cross) and *gestures* (e.g. blessing oneself) when they are worshipping, *to represent and communicate ideas* they hold and share about God.

- A visual image or gesture with *only one* meaning is called a *sign*. For example, on entering a Catholic church one is expected to *genuflect* before sitting down as a sign of respect for God.

- A visual image or gesture with more than one meaning is called a *symbol*. For example:

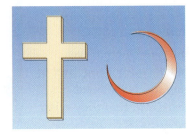

[The Cross]
Jesus died on the cross, the normal method of execution in the Roman Empire at that time. It was a shameful and painful death, but Christians believe that through it God showed his power over shame, pain, and death.

[The Crescent]
Muslims say that Islam guides a person's life just as the moon and stars guide a traveller in the desert. This symbol on a country's flag often indicates a Muslim state.

Introduction to Religion

QUESTIONS

(1) What is *religion*?

(2) What does it mean to believe something?

(3) What is faith? Give an example of an act of faith.

(4) What is organised religion?

(5) What does it mean to worship God?

(6) Name the founder of each of the following:
- Buddhism
- Sikhism
- Christianity
- Hinduism
- Islam
- Judaism

(7) What are *rituals*?

(8) Why do members of a religion use particular visual images and gestures when they worship God?

(9) What is a *sign*?

(10) What is a *symbol*?

(11) Explain the meaning of (a) the cross and (b) the crescent.

God

Buddhists do not worship any God. Buddha neither claimed to be a God nor wanted to be worshipped as one. *Hindus*, in contrast, worship a wide variety of gods and goddesses.

Most religions, however, believe in one supreme being. *Jews, Christians, Muslims* and *Sikhs* all believe in one God only. They believe that God is

- a pure spirit (i.e. *a being who does not have a physical body*)
- all-knowing
- all-powerful
- everywhere
- eternal
- unchanging
- creator of the world and
- the one who guides human destiny.

However, whether they worship one God (i.e. *monotheism*) or many gods (i.e. *polytheism*), those who sincerely hold religious beliefs agree that these beliefs are *central* to their whole way of life and are *not* some kind of added extra. They draw the strength and inspiration needed to face life's challenges

God as a loving parent.

from their faith in God. They believe that without God life would be meaningless and that there would be no hope of life after death.

Christians believe that God is a *person*, someone to whom people can *relate*, someone who *cares* more deeply for each of us than even the very best parents do for their children. However, it is important to bear in mind that, while God is often referred to as '*he*', Christians believe that *God is neither male nor female*.

Revelation

If left to our own devices, human beings would know very little about God. This is because God is so utterly different from anything else in our experience. For example, as human beings *we live in time*, in a world dominated by the ticking of the clock. But *God does not*. How can we hope to *adequately describe* a being who is *eternal*, i.e. lives outside of time? It has been remarked that we can no more imagine a being like God than a baby in his mother's womb can imagine her face.

So why, then, do Christians, for example, believe that God loves each human being and *invites* all to enter into a relationship of love and trust? How did they discover this? The answer is *they did not*. In common with Jews, Muslims and Sikhs, Christians believe that *God reached out to human beings* and *revealed things about his nature that otherwise we could never know*.

This is called God's *revelation*. The sacred books of each religion offer their own particular account of this.

While not denying any truths found in other religions, Christians believe that God has *most fully* revealed himself to human beings through the life, death and resurrection of *Jesus Christ*.

Sacred texts

Each of the major world religions has its own sacred writings or *scriptures*, which

- *set out their understanding of who God is* and
- *offer guidance about how they should live.*

These scriptures are treated with great respect.

The holy book of Islam is the *Qur'an* (pronounced Koran). The sacred book of Christians is *the Bible*.

The Bible

The word Bible comes from the Greek word '*biblia*' meaning 'books'. The Bible is not really one book but an entire *library* of books, numbering 73 in all, which have been bound together in a single volume.

The Bible is divided into two parts:

- *the Old Testament* = 46 books.
- *the New Testament* = 27 books.

FINDING A BIBLE REFERENCE

There is a code for finding your place in any book of the Bible.

This is the name of the particular book.

Note how each book is divided up into numbered 'chapters' — this number tells you which chapter to read.

Meaning: Here God's love is compared to the deep love a mother has for her child.

Isaiah 66:12-13

Each chapter is split up into numbered 'verses'— two numbers with a dash between means you have to read all the verses from the first number to the second.

Person swearing on a bible in court.

The word '*testament*' is derived from the Latin '*testamentum*' which means '*covenant*', i.e. a solemn and binding agreement between two parties, in this case God and human beings.

In the *Old Testament*, the people of God are the Jews. In the *New Testament*, Jesus makes it clear that all nations are God's people if they live according to God's ways. It is the birth of Jesus which marks the beginning of the *New Testament* or covenant between God and *all* people.

Jesus

No other person in human history has attracted more attention and interest than Jesus Christ. People of all religions, as well as those who are members of none, have been fascinated by his story.

Though Jesus never travelled far, never achieved great political power nor amassed a vast fortune, and died while still a young man, his impact on the history of our world since has been enormous. Just consider:

- Today Christianity, the religion he founded, is numerically the largest religion in the world, with approximately two billion members.

- We date the years of our world's history from Jesus' birth:
  B.C. = *before Christ*
  A.D. = *Anno Domini*, a Latin phrase meaning '*In the year of our Lord*'.

- No other figure in history has been the focus of more discussion or the subject of more works of art than Jesus.

Jesus on the cross ➡

Introduction to Religion

QUESTIONS

(1) Which major world religion does not worship a God or gods?

(2) Which major world religions worship (a) many gods and (b) one God only?

(3) Explain the meaning of the following terms: (a) *monotheism* and (b) *polytheism*.

(4) What role does God play in the life of someone who sincerely holds religious beliefs?

(5) '*If left to our own devices, human beings would know very little about God.*' Why is this so? Explain your answer.

(6) What do Christians, Jews, Muslims and Sikhs believe about *God's revelation*?

(7) What do Christians believe about Jesus Christ?

(8) Why does each major world religion have its own sacred writings or scriptures?

(9) What is the holy book of (a) *Islam* and (b) *Christianity*?

(10) What does the word '*bible*' mean?

(11) Name the two parts of the Bible. How many books are there in each?

(12) Explain the meaning of the word '*testament*' as used in the Bible.

(13) What event marks the beginning of the *New Testament*?

(14) Explain the letters B.C. and A.D.

(15) '*The impact of Jesus on world history has been enormous.*' What is the evidence offered to support this statement?

Jesus looking out across water.

CHAPTER TWO

THE SOURCES

Introduction

Jesus did not leave us a written account of his life and teachings. Our sources of information about Jesus are the writings of his Christian followers and the writings of a few Jewish and Roman commentators.

Setting aside the Christian sources for the moment, let us first consider what non-Christians have written about Jesus Christ.

Jewish sources

- The Jewish *Talmud* (an ancient commentary on Jewish teachings) contains references to Jesus, his disciples and teaching. However, he is described as a false teacher who was put to death on the eve of the Jewish feast of Passover.
- In his book *The Antiquities of the Jews*, written around A.D. 90, the historian Josephus describes Jesus as a wise teacher and miracle worker who won over many Jews and *gentiles (i.e. non-Jews)*. He says that Jesus was condemned to death by Pontius Pilate and that his followers believed that Jesus rose from the dead.

▲ Man writing a document with a quill and ink.

Roman sources

- Pliny, a Roman Governor in Asia Minor, wrote a letter in A.D. 110 to the Emperor Trajan complaining about the Christians in his area, who, he wrote, sang '*hymns to Christ as to a god*'.

- In his *Annals*, the historian Tacitus writing about A.D. 115, states that Jesus was a trouble-maker who was executed on the orders of Pontius Pilate during the reign of Emperor Tiberius.

While Jewish and Roman writers all testify to the fact that Jesus did exist and founded a new religion, they provide us with few details. We must turn to the writings of those who were most interested in Jesus' life and teachings — his Christian followers — if we want to find out more.

Christian sources

Before the death of those who had known Jesus, accounts of his life and of the spread of the new religion he founded were recorded and compiled to form the *New Testament*. This was written between A.D. 50 and 100. It consists of:

- *The Gospels* which record Jesus' life and teachings as remembered by those who knew him, for the guidance of the early Christians. There are four: Mark, Matthew, Luke and John.
- *The Acts of the Apostles* which describe the rapid spread of Christianity beyond Palestine.
- *The Epistles*, letters written by the leaders of the early Christian churches offering guidance to their communities, encouraging them to remain faithful, resolving disputes and clarifying Christian teachings.
- *The Book of Revelation* (or *Apocalypse*), a series of visions depicting the battle between the forces of good and evil, which predict the triumph of God and the final judgement of humanity at the end of time.

▲ Shelf containing books from the *New Testament*.

QUESTIONS

(1) List the four non-Christian sources of written information about Jesus.

(2) What information about Jesus can be extracted from these non-Christian sources?

(3) What is the *New Testament*?

(4) List the four parts of the *New Testament* and write a brief description of each.

CHAPTER THREE

THE GOSPELS I

▲ A Jewish scholar.

Introduction

The *New Testament* begins with the four Gospels. The word *gospel* is derived from the Old English *God-spell* meaning *good news*. The very word itself reflects the Christian understanding of the importance of Jesus. Christians believe that Jesus has brought the good news that God loves each and every human being and that each one is invited to share eternal life with God.

The authors

Since earliest times, Christians have associated the four Gospels with the names of *Mark*, *Matthew*, *Luke* and *John*. There are good reasons for accepting them as the authors though some scholars have voiced reservations.

Each author offers a different version of the *same* story:
- Mark was a companion of Paul (see *Acts* 12:12) who is thought to have accompanied Peter to Rome.
- Matthew was a tax collector whom Jesus chose as one of his twelve apostles (see *Matthew* 10:3).
- Luke was a Greek doctor who was a friend of Paul (see *Colossians* 4:14 and 2 *Timothy* 4:11).
- John, son of Zebedee, was the youngest and perhaps closest friend to Jesus among the twelve apostles (*Matthew* 17:1 and *John* 13:23).

The Gospel writers are also referred to as the four *evangelists* (meaning: *proclaimers of the good news*).

Matthew: a man
Mark: a lion
Luke: a bull
John: an eagle

▲ Each of the four evangelists is associated with a particular symbol, each based on a figure mentioned in the *Old Testament* book of *Ezekiel*.

Inspired by God

Jesus seems to have taught only by word of mouth, not by writing. How much, then, of the teaching recorded in the Gospels is actually Jesus' own words, and how much is put into his mouth by the four evangelists? This is a difficult question and scholars disagree among themselves on how to answer it.

Christians believe that the Bible is *the inspired word of God*. This does not necessarily mean, however, that Jesus' words are recorded in the Gospels exactly as he said them. Christians believe that while God inspired the evangelists, God did not directly tell them what to write. Rather God guided them to use their human talents and the normal means of communication to record faithfully the <u>meaning</u> of what Jesus said.

For example, it is quite acceptable today for a TV news programme to report some important person's speech, not in that person's actual words, but in the words of the reporter. While the reporter may not use exactly the same words as the person who made the speech, he/she will try to communicate accurately the *meaning* of what was said in the speech.

It was just the same in Jesus' time. The evangelists frequently reported the <u>message</u> of Jesus rather than the exact literal way in which he said it. Christians believe that God inspired the evangelists to be faithful to what Jesus taught.

Further, it is pointed out that the four Gospels have their source in the life and words of <u>one</u> person. Behind these four accounts is a teacher of great genius. <u>Jesus</u> is the source of the Gospels' teachings, not some committee of writers. The author of *Matthew* tells us that Jesus taught the people *'with authority'* (*Matthew* 7:29). This authority shines through every aspect of the four Gospels.

The Gospels are accepted by Christians as <u>substantially reliable records of what Jesus taught</u>.

DATES

It is difficult to give precise dates for the writing of the Gospels. The following are the dates accepted by many Christian scripture scholars:

c. A.D. 30	The death and resurrection of Jesus. Christians began preaching the good news to both Jews and gentiles.
30–50	The sayings of Jesus were handed on mainly by word of mouth.
50–64	The sayings of Jesus were collected and written down.
64	The Gospel of Mark was written.
70–80	The Gospels of Matthew, Luke and the Acts of the Apostles were written.
90	The Gospel of John was written.

The four Gospels were all written, therefore, before the end of the first century A.D. and so within the possible lifetime of eyewitnesses and certainly within the lifetime of those who knew the apostles.

QUESTIONS

(1) Explain the origin and meaning of the word *Gospel*.

(2) What is the meaning of the word *evangelist*?

(3) Name the four evangelists.

(4) What do Christians mean when they say that the Gospels are *the inspired word of God*?

(5) If the evangelists may not have always recorded the exact words of Jesus every time, what was their main aim when writing their accounts?

(6) Why do Christians believe that the four Gospels have their source in the life and words of one person?

(7) When were each of the four Gospels written?

(8) Why is it important that the four Gospels were written before the end of the first century A.D.?

(9) Identify the figure associated with each of the four evangelists.

The nature of the Gospels

A reader of the Gospels will quickly discover that they are not diaries of day to day events in Jesus' life. They do not offer us a biography (i.e. life-story) of Jesus in the modern sense of the word. The Gospels do not include a description of what Jesus looked like, nor do they tell us about his schooldays.

The reason for this is that the evangelists never intended to write down the complete life-story of Jesus. So they were not interested in recording the kind of personal details which might interest the modern reader. Rather, the Gospel authors were more concerned with explaining the *meaning* and *importance* of Jesus' life.

The evangelists believed that Jesus is *the Son of God* and wrote their Gospels to help others to believe this too. They recorded only what they considered to be the *vital* facts about Jesus. That is why, although *Matthew* and *Luke* briefly treat the events surrounding Jesus' birth, the main focus of all four Gospel writers is on Jesus' miracles, teachings, death and resurrection.

All About Faith

Why the Gospels were written

The early Christian community needed to compile and record accurately the sayings of Jesus and any important stories about him for several reasons:

- As time passed, those Christians who had known Jesus began to die. There was a fear that vital information might be lost. So Christians began to collect the sayings of Jesus and to write them down. Many scholars believe that the teachings of Jesus were put into collections some years before the Gospels were written. One of these early collections has been identified and named *Q* (from the German word *Quelle* meaning *Source*). The Gospel writers are thought to have consulted such collections.

- The Gospel accounts explained the meaning of Christianity to interested people and corrected any mistaken ideas about what Christians believed.

- They provided readings for use at Christian worship. To the present day the Christian Churches give priority or a special place of honour to the Gospels over the other parts of the *New Testament* because the Gospels are our principal sources of information about the life of Jesus.

QUESTIONS

(1) Do the Gospel writers offer us biographies of Jesus in the modern sense of the word? Explain your answer.

(2) What was the main concern of the evangelists?

(3) On what parts of Jesus' story did the evangelists mainly focus?

(4) What was 'Q' and how did it help the evangelists?

(5) Why did early Christian communities want to record the story and teachings of Jesus?

CHAPTER FOUR

THE GOSPELS II

The earliest manuscripts

We do *not* possess a complete original manuscript of the *New Testament* that dates from the first century a.d. Our modern printed *New Testament* is based on later copies of the original documents. The earliest complete manuscript of the *New Testament* is the *Codex Sinaiticus*, which was preserved in the monastery of St. Catherine in the Sinai Desert and which dates from the fourth century A.D.

This raises a question: are the Gospel accounts we have today the same as the original ones written in the first century A.D.?

Genuine copies?

Modern Christian scholars believe that they <u>are</u> genuine for the following reasons:

▲ Folio from St. John's Gospel.
Greek codex of the Bible, fourth century.

▲ Rylands Papyrus.

■ The Christian copyists of the *New Testament* believed that Jesus was *the Son of God*. Consequently, the idea of faithfully copying out the details of Jesus' story as set down in the original *Gospel* manuscripts would have been a matter of the utmost seriousness for them and the Christian communities in which they lived. The evangelists were believed to have been inspired by God and so any attempt to alter their original texts would have been totally rejected.

- Archaeologists have discovered fragments of copies of the *New Testament* that were produced before the *Codex Sinaiticus*. The earliest known <u>undisputed</u> fragment is a section of the Gospel of *John* known as the *Rylands Papyrus* which dates from A.D. 134. Scholars have used these early fragments to act as a 'spot-check' to confirm that our modern copies of the *New Testament* are reliable and accurate.

- Further, these early surviving fragments of copies of the *New Testament* from the second and third centuries A.D. were all discovered in <u>different places</u>, yet all contain <u>matching</u> material. This supports the view that all these fragments had a *common* original manuscript source which has since been lost. Where there is much material in common between these fragments it is a good indicator that they are genuine copies.

Conclusion

As a result, most scholars accept that we now possess accurate reproductions of the lost original *New Testament* manuscripts.

QUESTIONS

(1) What is the name given to the oldest known *complete manuscript* of the *New Testament*? Where was it discovered?

(2) What is the name given to the *earliest* known *fragment* of the *New Testament*?

(3) Why do most modern Christian scholars believe that we possess accurate and reliable copies of the original *New Testament*?

Why four?

Christians believe that there is really only *one* Gospel (Good News) but that the early Christians just produced *four different versions of it*. Why?

By the time the Gospels came to be written in the latter half of the first century A.D., there were Christian communities scattered across the Middle East, North Africa and Southern Europe. Each community had to cope with its own particular set of challenges. Each evangelist wrote his own version of

Jesus' story to help his own community cope with the particular problems it faced.

For example:

- If one reads *Mark*, the shortest Gospel, one will notice how he devotes almost a quarter of his Gospel to recounting the story of Jesus' suffering, trial and death. Scholars believe that Mark wrote his version of Jesus' story partly with the intention of giving encouragement to Christians at a time when they were being persecuted by the Romans.
- There are a great many references to the *Old Testament* in the Gospel of *Matthew*. This evangelist seems to assume that his readers have already studied the *Old Testament* and know it well.

  Matthew probably wrote his Gospel to help people in his community who had <u>converted</u> (i.e. changed) from Judaism to Christianity. He wanted to help them understand the meaning of Jesus' life and what they would be expected to believe.
- Of all the Gospels, the Gospel of *Luke* offers us the fullest account of Jesus' life. It forms the first half of an unfinished history of Christianity's beginnings. The second half of the story is recorded in *The Acts of the Apostles*, also written by the same author.

  Luke was the only Gospel to have been written by a *gentile* (i.e. a non-Jew) and was written particularly to explain Jesus' life and teachings to other gentiles who had become Christians. He devotes much of his Gospel to showing how Jesus loved the poor, the sick and the helpless, and how God is always ready to forgive. *Luke* was concerned to show that Jesus is the *saviour and friend* of all people, *Jews and non-Jews*.
- The Gospel of *John* was the last one to be written. Its author seems to assume that his readers already know the details of Jesus' life. *John* does *not* include any of *the parables* (i.e. *stories with a moral message*) which are recorded in the other Gospels. He does record some of Jesus' miracles. However, *John* is more concerned with the question of who Jesus is and why people should live like him. This is because, by the time this Gospel came to be written, these were the questions that were important for Christians. *John* also wanted to reassure Christians that Jesus is alive and with us now.

QUESTIONS

(1) What do Christians believe about the Gospel?
(2) Why did each evangelist write his own version of Jesus' story?
(3) Which Gospel offers the fullest account of Jesus' life?
(4) Which Gospel was the last to be written?
(5) What was the intention behind *Mark's* Gospel?
(6) What does *Matthew* seem to assume about his readers?
(7) Why did *Matthew* write his Gospel?
(8) Which other *New Testament* book was written by the author of *Luke*?
(9) For whom did *Luke* write his Gospel?
(10) What kind of person was Jesus, according to *Luke*?
(11) State one way in which *John's* Gospel is different from the other three.
(12) Why did *John* write his Gospel?

Parallel passages

Read the following extracts from three different Gospels:

> *'Then he called the crowd to him along with his disciples and said: 'If anyone would come after me, he must deny himself and take up his cross and follow me. For whoever wants to save his life will lose it, but whoever loses his life for me and for the gospel will save it.*
> *What good is it for a man to gain the whole world, yet forfeit his soul? Or what can a man give in exchange for his soul? If anyone is ashamed of me and my words in this adulterous and sinful generation, the Son of Man will be ashamed of him when he comes in his Father's glory with the holy angels.'*
> *And he said to them, 'I tell you the truth, some who are standing here will not taste death before they see the kingdom of God come with power.'*
> Mark 8:34–9:1

> *Then Jesus said to his disciples, 'If anyone would come after me, he must deny himself and take up his cross and follow me. For whoever wants to save his life will lose it, but whoever loses his life for me will find it. What good will it be for a man if he gains the whole world, yet forfeits his soul? Or what can a man give in*

exchange for his soul? For the Son of Man is going to come in his Father's glory with his angels, and then he will reward each person according to what he has done. I tell you the truth, some who are standing here will not taste death before they see the Son of Man coming in his kingdom.'
Matthew 16:24–28

Then he said to them all: 'If anyone would come after me, he must deny himself and take up his cross daily and follow me. For whoever wants to save his life will lose it, but whoever loses his life for me will save it. What good is it for a man to gain the whole world, and yet lose or forfeit his very self? If anyone is ashamed of me and my words, the Son of Man will be ashamed of him when he comes in his glory and in the glory of the Father and of the holy angels. I tell you the truth, some who are standing here will not taste death before they see the kingdom of God.'
Luke 9:23–27

These extracts are so alike that it seems that someone is copying from someone else! One can find many examples of such parallel passages in the Gospels of *Mark*, *Matthew* and *Luke*, which largely agree in:

- their basic outline of the main events in Jesus' life;
- the sequence in which they organise these events;
- their wording of many of Jesus' statements.

It is because they share so many similarities that *Mark*, *Matthew* and *Luke* are called the Synoptic Gospels ('synoptic' meaning 'seen together')

Why is this the case?

Consider the following diagram:

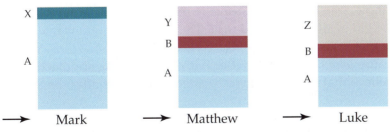

Notice how the three Synoptic Gospels share the identical material marked [A] above. This is because *Mark* was the first Gospel to be written and both *Matthew* and *Luke* included material written by *Mark* in their accounts of Jesus' life.

Differences

However, despite so much common material, differences remain between the three Synoptic Gospels. For example:

- Some events are placed in a different order.
- Each Gospel mentions events and records statements made by Jesus which the others do not. For example, only *Matthew* and *Luke* offer any information about Jesus' birth, while *Mark* says nothing at all on this topic. However, only *Luke* records the story of how Jesus, as a twelve-year-old boy, became separated from Mary and Joseph while in Jerusalem.

Why differences?

Again, consult the diagram on page 19. You will see that both *Matthew* and *Luke* share a common source marked (B) above. Scholars believe both of them consulted a long-since-lost collection of Jesus' sayings now known as the 'Q' document (from the German '*Quelle*' meaning 'source'). *Mark* did not use the Q document when composing his account.

Also you will see that each of the three Gospels included material not found in the others and marked (X), (Y) and (Z) above. This was probably drawn from other eyewitness accounts.

This helps to explain the differences between the three Synoptic Gospels.

John's Gospel

John's Gospel is quite different in style and emphasis from the Synoptics:

- *John* did not copy material from either *Mark* or the Q document.
- *John* only recorded certain events and sayings of Jesus because he was mainly interested in explaining important truths about who Jesus is, rather than what he did.

For example, *John* is the only Gospel to record the story of how Jesus restores the gift of sight to a blind man. This is because John wanted to help people see that Jesus is '*the light of the world*'.

It is because *John* takes such a reflective, deep-thinking approach that scholars believe that this Gospel was written some years after the Synoptics.

QUESTIONS

(1) What is the meaning of the word *Synoptic*?

(2) Name the three Synoptic Gospels.

(3) In what ways are they similar?

(4) Which evangelists included material first recorded by *Mark* in their Gospels?

(5) What are the differences between the Synoptic Gospels?

(6) What is the importance of the 'Q' document?

(7) Which Synoptic Gospel did not use Q?

(8) In what ways is *John's* Gospel different from the Synoptics?

CHAPTER FIVE

THE SETTING

Introduction

Before we begin studying the life of Jesus we need first to learn about the place and time in which Jesus was born and where his extraordinary story unfolded. Thanks to the pain-staking research of generations of archaeologists and historians, we can build up a highly detailed and generally reliable picture of what life was like in the time of Jesus.

Name

The land in which Jesus was born has had many names down through the centuries. Today it is known as <u>Israel</u> (meaning 'God strives') the name given to Jacob, one of the founders of the Jewish race (*Genesis* 32:27–28). Israel now is an independent, self-governing state, but two thousand years ago it was merely one province of the vast Roman empire, which had conquered the area in 63 B.C. Then it was called <u>Palestine</u>, a name taken from the Philistines, an ancient people who had once occupied the area. This is the name which will be used in the following pages.

The Roman Empire in the first century A.D.

Position

Palestine has been described as merely '*a strip of land between sea and desert*'. It is part of what is known as the fertile crescent, a well-watered area which sweeps in a huge semi-circle from the Persian gulf shores of Iraq in the east, northwards through Syria, then down southwards through Palestine and onto the Nile valley of Egypt in the west. South of this fertile crescent lies the Arabian desert. Palestine lies on the edge of the western arc of the crescent, hemmed in by the Mediterranean on one side and the desert on the other.

QUESTIONS

(1) Explain the meaning of the name given to the modern state of *Israel*.

(2) From where was the name *Palestine* taken?

(3) What is the *fertile crescent*?

(4) Why has Palestine been described as '*a strip of land between sea and desert*'?

Size

Palestine measured just 150 miles in length and anywhere from 30 miles to 50 miles in width from its western coast to its eastern border. Its total area was only about 7,000 square miles, making it no bigger than the present-day province of Leinster. Today, this whole area can easily be travelled from one end to the other by car in just a few hours. Indeed, a Jewish person in the time of Jesus could have walked the same journey in less than five days.

Landscape and climate

The landscape and climate of Palestine have changed little since the time of Jesus. The terrain falls into three almost parallel zones. From west to east they are:

- the coastal plain
- the western hills
- the rift valley through which the Jordan flows

To the east of this lies a great plateau and beyond this and to the south there are vast expanses of scorching desert.

There are basically two seasons in Palestine: the hot, dry summer (May to September) and the cool, wet winter (October to April).

Land of contrasts

Though small in size, Palestine remains a land of remarkably diverse landscapes:

- The area around the Dead Sea in the south has temperatures reaching 50 degrees celcius.
- In contrast, the land around the Sea of Galilee in the north is generally green and fertile. This area remains home to many thriving farming and fishing communities.

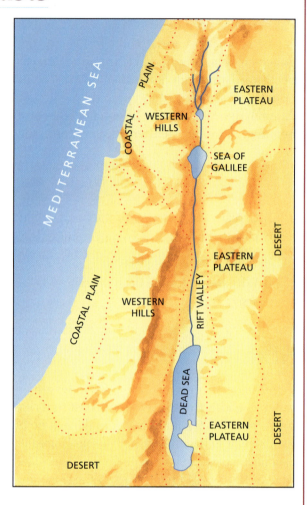

Natural regions of Palestine.

QUESTIONS

(1) What was the size of Palestine?

(2) Describe the terrain and climate of Palestine.

(3) Is it true to say that Palestine is a land of great contrasts? Give reasons for your answer.

CHAPTER SIX

THE CHOSEN PEOPLE I

Introduction

If we are to understand the life and work of Jesus, then we need to learn more about the people among whom he grew up and to whom he devoted his life. In particular, we need to examine the events and experiences that made the Jews the kind of people they were.

▲ Reflecting on the word of God.

The *Old Testament*

The Jews who lived in Palestine at the time of Jesus were very proud of their history. It showed that, in spite of all the hardships and suffering they had endured, the Jews had continued to believe in God and had struggled to live according to God's laws.

In the beginning, the Jews kept their history alive by passing on important stories and teachings from one generation to the next by word of mouth (i.e. by *oral tradition*). Eventually Jewish scholars began to write these stories down and their different books were later gathered together to form what Christians call the *Old Testament*.

The successive generations of Jewish scholars who wrote the *Old Testament* all shared a common purpose *to show that every event in the story of their people had a meaning and a purpose because it was all part of God's plan for the Jews and for the whole world.*

All About Faith

> ## QUESTIONS
>
> (1) Why were the Jews proud of their history?
> (2) What is meant by *'oral tradition'*?
> (3) What is the *Old Testament*?
> (4) What was the common purpose of the authors of the *Old Testament*?

The patriarchs

Every <u>devout</u> Jew (i.e. one who takes his/her religion seriously) is familiar with the stories about the great people and events which are recorded in the *Old Testament*. The Jews trace their origin as a distinct people to about 1900 B.C. when the era of the patriarchs began (*Genesis* 12–50). Abraham is recognised as the first *patriarch* (i.e. <u>founding father</u>) of the Jewish people or, as they were originally known, *the Hebrews*.

Around 2000 B.C. the Hebrews were just a small group of travelling merchants who led long trains of camels and donkeys loaded down with goods from one trading post to another. This was the source of their name. As they walked, their leather sandals and their animals' hooves kicked up a lot of dust which settled on them. Other people began calling them *Abiru*, meaning 'dusty ones'. In time *Abiru* became *Hebrew*.

According to *Genesis* 12:1–5 Abraham was inspired by God to lead a small group of Hebrews across the fertile crescent from Ur in Mesopotamia to settle in the <u>land of Canaan</u> (i.e. Palestine).

▲ God calls Abraham.

The covenant

According to *Genesis*, chapters 15 and 17, God made a <u>covenant</u> (i.e. *a holy agreement*) with Abraham and his descendants. *If they faithfully worshipped him and kept his laws then he would guarantee their ownership of Palestine.* The Hebrews were God's 'chosen people'. This did *not* mean that God was declaring them to be better than any other people. Rather, that God had selected them and invited them to fulfil a special <u>mission</u>: to reveal to the world that there was only *one God* and to offer good example so as to lead others to love and worship God.

The God of the Hebrews

The God of the Hebrews was utterly unlike any god worshipped elsewhere at that time. The gods of the Egyptians and Mesopotamians behaved like humans but were far more powerful. These gods were usually *feared* rather than respected. This was because the Egyptians and Mesopotamians believed that their gods would act in cruel and wicked ways whenever they were in a bad mood!

In contrast to this, the God of the Hebrews used his power *only* to do what was *good and just*. Their God was all-knowing, all-powerful and worthy of their love and respect.

QUESTIONS

(1) What does the word *devout* mean when used in relation to a person's attitude to his/her religion?

(2) What does the word *patriarch* mean? Who was the first patriarch?

(3) By what name were the Jews originally known? How did they become known by that name?

(4) Why did Abraham lead his followers to Canaan?

(5) What is a *covenant*?

(6) Describe the covenant God made with Abraham.

(7) What is meant by describing the Hebrews as God's *chosen people*?

(8) Compare the gods of the Egyptians and Mesopotamians with the God of the Hebrews.

From guests to slaves

When Abraham and his followers settled in Palestine, they had hoped to build a better life there. However, their descendants had to endure great hardships caused by long droughts which ruined their crops and devastated the grasslands which supported their livestock. While some Hebrews chose to remain in Palestine, most opted to migrate into the fertile Nile Delta region of Egypt which was rich in grain, around 1700 B.C.

At first the Hebrews were made welcome and the pharaohs (i.e. Egyptian kings) employed them as craftsmen. Then Egypt was invaded and partly

▲ Joseph welcomes his brothers to Egypt.

occupied by *the Hyksos*, a people from central Asia. The Hebrews welcomed the Hyksos and enjoyed some prosperity under their rule. However, during the reign of Pharaoh Ahmose I (c. 1570–1550 B.C.) the Hyksos were expelled from Egypt. The Hebrews then paid the price for supporting the losing side. They were forced into slavery.

For the next three centuries the Hebrews in Egypt suffered terrible hardships. Those who had remained in Palestine struggled to survive its harsh climate and the frequent attacks of hostile tribes. The one thing that kept the Hebrews going, however, was their unique and deep faith. They were the *only* people on earth at that time who believed in and worshipped *one* God alone. They trusted that God would not desert them. They were not disappointed. God, they believed, had finally sent them someone who would lead them to freedom — Moses.

Moses

The story of Moses can be found in the *Old Testament* books of *Exodus* and *Deuteronomy*. They portray Moses as a man of great intelligence and goodness.

Moses had an extraordinary experience of the power and mystery of God which changed his whole outlook on life. God appeared to Moses in the form of a bush which was on fire but did not burn (*Exodus* 3:1–20). After this Moses found that his trust in God gave him the courage to lead the movement seeking freedom for the Hebrews. God called on Moses to lead his chosen people back to the *promised land* — Palestine.

▲ Moses and the burning bush.

The exodus

According to the *Old Testament*, God gave Moses the power to make miracles (*Exodus* 4:1–17). Moses confronted the pharaoh, whom some scholars believe was Rameses II, and demanded that he set the Hebrews free (*Exodus* 5:1–5). When the pharaoh refused, Egypt was struck by a series of disasters (*Exodus* 7:8–12:42). These events shattered the confidence of the pharaoh and about 1250 b.c. he finally gave in, allowing the Hebrews to leave Egypt altogether. This great movement of the Hebrew people back to Palestine is called <u>the exodus</u> (meaning: <u>the going forth</u>).

QUESTIONS

(1) What event led many Hebrews to move from Palestine to Egypt?

(2) Why were the Hebrews forced into slavery by the Egyptians?

(3) What belief kept the Hebrews going despite all the hardships they endured?

(4) Where can we find the *Old Testament* account of Moses' life?

(5) What impact did God's appearance in *Exodus* 3:1–20 have on Moses?

(6) What happened when the pharaoh refused to free the Jews?

(7) Why did the pharaoh change his mind, set the Hebrews free and allow them to return to Palestine?

(8) What is the meaning of the word *exodus*?

The Law of God

The exodus was the most important event in Hebrew history. While journeying home to the promised land, the Hebrews had to pass through the harsh, scorching terrain of the Sinai desert.

According to the *Old Testament*, it was during this journey that God inspired the Hebrews to draw up a detailed code setting out how they should live. This is known as the *Torah* (meaning: <u>the Law</u>) and it can be found in the books of *Genesis*, *Exodus*, *Leviticus*, *Numbers* and *Deuteronomy*. All these rules, however, were summarised in ten short and simple laws which, they believed, God himself gave to Moses while he was fasting and praying on Mount Sinai. They have been known ever since as the *Ten Commandments* and they are at the very heart of not just the Jewish religion, but Christianity and Islam as well.

All About Faith

THE COMMANDMENTS

1. I am the Lord your God. Do not worship anyone but me.
2. You must not use the name of the Lord your God in vain.
3. Remember to observe the Sabbath as a holy day.
4. Honour your father and your mother.
5. You must not commit murder.
6. You must not commit adultery.
7. You must not steal.
8. You must not tell lies.
9. You must not covet your neighbour's wife.
10. You must not covet your neighbour's property.

(see *Deuteronomy* 5:1–22)

Mount Sinai at sunrise.

Renewing the covenant

God gave the Hebrews this opportunity to renew the *covenant* (i.e. holy agreement) he had made with their founding-father Abraham centuries before. This was a very important moment in Hebrew history. The descendants of Abraham freely chose to re-new their commitment to honour (i.e. live up to) the agreement their ancestors had made with God. God promised them the land of Palestine but in return the Hebrews promised God to keep his commandments faithfully. They promised to fulfil their mission to reveal to the whole world the goodness and greatness of God.

QUESTIONS

(1) What is *the Torah*?
(2) What was the whole purpose of the *Ten Commandments*?
(3) List and learn the *Ten Commandments*.
(4) When the Hebrews chose to re-new the covenant God had made with their ancestors, what did they commit themselves to do?

CHAPTER SEVEN

THE CHOSEN PEOPLE II

Israel established

For almost two hundred years after they had reached the promised land, the Hebrews had to fight a series of wars before they gained control of the area. Throughout those years they were sustained by their desire to build a strong, secure homeland. A key element in achieving their victory was the decision to unite the different tribes under one leader. Saul was the first king. He was succeeded by David who finally led the Hebrews to victory (*1 Samuel* 16:1–31:13 and *2 Samuel* 1:1–8:18).

Around 1000 B.C. David established a united Hebrew state with its capital city at Jerusalem. The Hebrews called their new kingdom Israel.

Bernini's statue of the young David (17th Century).

David and Solomon

The Hebrews in later times would look back to the days when David and later Solomon ruled Israel as the most glorious period in their history. David shrewdly took advantage of Egypt's temporary weakness and built up strong trade links and signed treaties with neighbouring people, such as the Phoenicians, to make Israel independent, secure and wealthy for a time.

After David's death about 970 B.C., he was succeeded by his son Solomon, who then built a magnificent temple in Jerusalem. This served as a resting place for the Ark of the Covenant, the casket in which, it was said, the stone tablets on which God had carved the *Ten Commandments* were kept.

Many Hebrews, however, grew unhappy with Solomon. They resented the harshness of his rule. Many did not like paying high taxes or working on his building projects. After Solomon died in 930 B.C. the kingdom split in two: with Israel to the north and a separate state called Judah, with its capital at Jerusalem in the south.

QUESTIONS

(1) Who was the first king of the Hebrews?

(2) Who established the first united Hebrew kingdom? When?

(3) Why, do you think, the Hebrews of later centuries considered the period when David and Solomon ruled Israel as the most glorious period in their people's history?

(4) What was the Ark of the Covenant?

(5) Why did many Hebrews grow dissatisfied with Solomon's rule?

(6) What happened to the kingdom after Solomon's death?

The prophets

Today, the word *prophet* is often used to describe someone who claims that he/she can accurately predict future events. For the ancient Hebrews, however, a prophet was *a holy man who had received messages from God which he then preached to the people.*

In the years following the division of the kingdom into two separate and often quarrelling states, a number of prophets, most notably Elijah, Amos, Hosea, Jeremiah, Ezekiel and Isaiah, came forward to offer guidance to the Hebrews.

These prophets:

- Criticised the way in which many Hebrews were living.
- Condemned the way the rich abused the poor.

Raphael's Isaiah (16th Century).

- Reminded the people of their duty to love God and do good to one another.
- Warned the Hebrews about the dangers of fighting among themselves.

A tempting target

The Hebrews had grown so pre-occupied with their petty squabbling that they had forgotten that, even when the two kingdoms had been united under David and Solomon, their land had always been a tempting target for their powerful neighbours.

Why? Though covering only a small area, the Hebrew kingdoms occupied a geographical position of great military and economic importance. Their land was the meeting point for three continents, a cross-roads where the great over-land trade routes of the ancient world, from Europe to the north, Asia to the east and Africa to the south, met.

Disaster

The Hebrews refused to listen to the prophets' warnings. After nearly two centuries of in-fighting, both kingdoms had been weakened and were surrounded by powerful neighbours. In 722 B.C. the Assyrians occupied Israel, killing or carrying away all its inhabitants as slaves. The Israelites, as the people of the northern kingdom were called, were scattered throughout the Assyrian empire and simply ceased to exist as a people, disappearing into the mists of time.

In 586 B.C. a Babylonian army overran the southern kingdom of Judah. Most of Judah's inhabitants, who were now known as *the Jews*, were marched away into exile to work as slaves in the great city of Babylon.

QUESTIONS

(1) What did the Hebrews believe about their prophets?
(2) What kind of things did the prophets criticise the Hebrews for doing?
(3) Why were the Hebrew kingdoms of Israel and Judah tempting targets for their powerful neighbours?
(4) What happened to the northern kingdom of Israel in 722 B.C.?
(5) What happened to the southern kingdom of Judah in 586 B.C.?
(6) By what name were the people of Judah known by then?

Captives in Babylon

The terrible events of the Babylonian conquest were burned deep into Jewish memory:

> *'Swifter than eagles swooping down from the sky,
> they
> chased us down.
> They tracked us down in the hills; they took us by
> surprise in the desert.'*
> Lamentations 4:19

▲ Jews being led away as slaves to Babylon.

The Babylonian army of Nebuchadnezzar razed Jerusalem and demolished the temple. They rounded up tens of thousands of Jews and force-marched them away to work as slave labour in the great city of Babylon.

While captives there, the Jews were made to re-think their attitudes to many things. Most immediately, they were forced by their new circumstances to drop the Hebrew language for everyday use and had to replace it with *Aramaic*, the language of their new masters. From then on, the Jews used Hebrew only for reciting formal prayers at religious ceremonies or when studying their sacred writings.

Since they were exiled far from their homeland and no longer had the temple of Solomon in which to worship God, the Jews were forced to make changes in their religion:

- They began meeting in small groups each *Sabbath* day (i.e. their day of rest) to pray and study their history and religion.
- From these meetings came the idea of a *synagogue*, i.e. a building in which a community of Jews gathered together to pray and encourage each other to practise their religion faithfully in daily life.
- To preserve their history and religious beliefs the Jews decided to collect and write down all their laws, sayings and stories on *scrolls*, (i.e. long rolls of parchment). These would be later used to write the different books which in time would be used to form the *Old Testament*.
- The study of these holy writings led the Jews to place a great value on learning and scholarship. Their teachers, whom they called *rabbis*, became important figures within each local community centred on their synagogue.

QUESTIONS

(1) With what language did the Jews replace Hebrew for day to day use once they were captive in Babylon?

(2) Why were the Jews forced to make changes in the way they practised their religion?

(3) What is the *Sabbath*?

(4) What is a *synagogue*?

(5) What are *scrolls*?

(6) Why did the Jews in Babylon collect and write down their laws and stories on scrolls?

(7) What is a *rabbi*?

CHAPTER EIGHT

AWAITING THE MESSIAH

Drawing lessons

Having suffered such a humiliating defeat at the hands of the Babylonians, with little prospect of ever regaining their freedom, it would have been quite tempting for the Jews to have given into cynicism and despair. After all, had not God promised to protect them? It seemed that God had deserted them in the time of their greatest need.

However, as the *Old Testament* shows, the Jewish people came to realise that they themselves, not God, were responsible for this disaster. God had been right and they wrong. God had sent the prophets to warn them but they had not listened. They came to see their enslavement as the result of their own foolishness.

> 'I stretch out my hands, and no one will help me . . . But the Lord is just, for I have disobeyed him.'
>
> Lamentations 1:18

Through all their terrible experiences, the Jews came to realise that God was much more than the protector of their nation. Their God stood for wisdom and justice. God would be faithful to them, but they in turn would have to be faithful to God. No matter how terrible the situation they were facing, they believed that it was part of God's plan for the world. They believed that God was guiding human history slowly but surely towards perfection and that they, the Jewish people, had an important role to play in bringing this about.

Obstacles

In 539 B.C. the Jews were unexpectedly freed from slavery and allowed to return home when Cyrus of Persia conquered Babylon. However, in the years following their return home, the Jews suffered many setbacks at the hands of successive conquerors: Persians, Greeks and Romans. The once great kingdom of David and Solomon was reduced to a pale shadow of its former glory. It was merely a small province of someone else's vast empire. The Jews themselves divided once more into rival groups. <u>They needed a leader.</u> The prophets told them that God had promised to send them one. They gave this promised leader the title *Messiah*.

◂ Jews rebuilding their homes after return from Babylonian exile.

QUESTIONS

(1) What lessons did the Jewish people learn from their defeat and enslavement by the Babylonians?

(2) What did they believe about God's plan for the world and the part they would play in it?

(3) Why did the Jews believe they needed a great leader?

(4) What did their prophets tell them about this?

(5) What title did they give this great leader?

The promised Messiah

The title Messiah comes from the Hebrew *Moshiach*, meaning *anointed one*. In Old Testament times, kings and high priests were anointed with oil to show that they had been chosen by God to fulfil an important task. For example, read this account of the anointing of King David:

> '*Samuel took the olive oil and anointed David where he stood with his brothers, and the spirit of God entered into David and stayed with him from that day on.*'
>
> 1 Samuel 16:13

All About Faith

The Jews looked back to David's time as a 'golden age' when they were a free and respected nation. By the first century a.d., most Jews hoped that the Messiah would be a warrior king who would:

- bring God's peace and justice among them
- free them from foreign domination
- set up a new Jewish kingdom even more glorious than that of David.

Devout Jews daily recited the following prayer:

> *'I believe with perfect faith in the coming of the Messiah and, even if he delay, still will I await his coming every day.'*

The Christ

When the Bible was first translated from Hebrew into Greek, the Greek word used in place of the Hebrew Messiah was *Christos*. From this we get the title Christ (also meaning 'anointed one'). So when someone says Jesus Christ it means Jesus the Messiah.

The Jewish people believe that the Messiah has yet to come. Christians, however, believe that in Jesus of Nazareth the Messiah/Christ *has arrived* and that he *will return again* at the end of time.

▲ Israel. Bedouin with sheep and goats.

QUESTIONS

(1) Explain the meaning of the title *Messiah*.
(2) What was the importance of anointing with oil?
(3) What kind of Messiah did most Jews hope God would send?
(4) Explain the origin and meaning of the title *Christ*.
(5) What do Jews and Christians believe about the Messiah?

CHAPTER NINE

THE BIRTH OF JESUS

The story

The story of Jesus' birth is one of the most memorable and attractive stories ever written, and has been the inspiration for many beautiful works of art. By combining materials from the Gospels of *Luke* and *Matthew* we can offer the following account:

Jesus was born during the reign of the Roman emperor, Augustus, who called a census of the Jews to find out which of them were eligible to pay taxes. Everyone had to state their name, social rank, occupation and so on, but they could not fill in their census details in the place where they normally lived. Instead, all Jews had to go to the place from which their family originally came. Joseph, husband of Mary, was a descendent of King David who came from Bethlehem. Mary and Joseph were forced to leave their home in Nazareth and travel to Bethlehem, and it was there that Jesus was born.

On the night of his birth, shepherds visited the infant Jesus and worshipped him. They were later followed by Magi (i.e. wise men) from the east who had followed a star, believing it would lead them to a great king whose birth they were expecting. They brought with them three gifts:

- Gold — a sign they recognised Jesus as a king.
- Frankincense — to show that they had come to worship Jesus.
- Myrrh — a warning that they believed Jesus would have to suffer much (*Matthew* 2:11).

◂ Botticelli's Adoration of the Magi (15th Century).

But the Magi were not the only ones seeking Jesus. Ever fearful of any threat to his throne, King Herod ordered his soldiers to kill all male children in Bethlehem aged two years or younger. However, Jesus, Mary and Joseph escaped this massacre and took refuge in Egypt. After Herod's death they returned to Nazareth, where Jesus grew up.

Naming the event

There are three names used by Christians for the birth of Jesus:
- *The Nativity* which is derived from the Latin *'natus'* meaning 'the birth',
- *Christmas* meaning 'Christ's mass' or 'Christ's festival',
- *The Incarnation* which means 'becoming flesh' and refers to the Christian belief that God actually became a human being in the person of Jesus.

Dating the event

We cannot say with certainty the exact date of Jesus' birth. This date was not recorded in the Gospels and early Christians did not come to realise its importance for some time. Only gradually did they realise that Jesus' birth had marked a whole new era in human history.

To show this clearly, the years before Jesus' birth were termed B.C. and those afterward A.D.

The task of working out the date of Jesus' birth was given to a monk named Denis. He is responsible for our current system of numbering the years taking the birth of Jesus as occurring in year A.D. 1. This system has been in use since the sixth century A.D. However, it is now generally acknowledged that Denis arrived at the <u>wrong date</u> for Jesus' birth. How?

It seems that Denis interpreted the statement that Jesus was 'about thirty years old when he began his ministry' (*Luke* 3:23) as though it meant he was exactly thirty years old. This led him to miscalculate. Scholars today believe that Jesus was born five or six years earlier than Denis had thought. Why?

Using the information contained in the Gospels and matching it with non-Christian sources we can see that the years 5 or 6 B.C. by our calendar are more likely dates for Jesus' birth:

- King Herod died in 4 B.C. Since he ordered all boys up to the age of two to be put to death (*Matthew* 2:16), this means that Jesus would have to have been born in either 5 or 6 B.C.
- Chinese astronomical records state that in the year 5 B.C., a brilliant star appeared in the eastern sky. Some scholars believe that this was a 'super nova', i.e. a brilliant light caused by an exploding star, and that this may be the origin of the Star of Bethlehem mentioned in *Matthew* 2:1–10.

The Birth of Jesus

Why December 25th?

The early Christians lived under Roman rule. Their Roman overlords worshipped many gods, but perhaps the most widely worshipped of these gods was Mithras, also known as *Sol Invicta* (meaning: 'the invincible sun'). Mithras' birth date was the 25th December and it was celebrated near the time of the winter solstice (i.e. the shortest day of the year). Because the hours of sunlight grow longer after the solstice, the Romans claimed that Mithras, the sun god, was regaining his strength.

When Christianity became the official religion of the Roman empire in the fourth century A.D., its leaders decided to take over this date. They considered it to be an appropriate date on which to celebrate Jesus' birth. This was because Christians believed that Jesus, not Mithras, is *'the rising sun from on high who has come to visit us'* (*Luke* 1:78) and that Jesus alone can be called *'the light of the world'* (*John* 9:5).

The Star of Bethlehem.

The fifth candle of the Advent Wreath being lit.

However, not all Christians accepted this date. Orthodox (eastern) Catholics chose a different date: the 6th January. They combined two important events in Jesus' life, his birth and his baptism, and celebrate them on the same day each year.

QUESTIONS

(1) Who was the Roman emperor when Jesus was born?

(2) Why did Mary and Joseph have to travel to Bethlehem for the census?

(3) Explain the meaning of each of the gifts given by the wise men.

(4) Why did Herod order the murder of all male children of two years and younger in Bethlehem?

(5) Explain each of the following:
- <u>Nativity</u>
- <u>Christmas</u>
- <u>Incarnation</u>.

(6) How did Denis arrive at the wrong date for the birth of Jesus?

(7) Why do modern scholars think that Jesus was most likely to have been born around 5 or 6 B.C.?

(8) By what other name did the Romans worship the god Mithras?

(9) Why did the Romans believe that Mithras' strength returned to him after the winter solstice?

(10) Why did Christians come to believe that December 25th was a more appropriate date than any other on which to celebrate Jesus' birth?

Points of agreement

The story of Jesus' birth is found in two Gospels: *Luke* and *Matthew*. They both agree on the following details:

Luke 1:5	The story is set during the reign of Herod the Great	*Matthew* 2:1
Luke 1:27, 2:5	Mary was a virgin who had been formally engaged to Joseph	*Matthew* 1:16
Luke 1:27, 2:4	Joseph was descended from King David	*Matthew* 1:16
Luke 2:7	Jesus was conceived in Mary's womb, not through sexual intercourse with Joseph, but through the power of God. This is called 'the virginal conception' or 'the virgin birth'	*Matthew* 1:18–20
Luke 2:7	Mary gave birth to Jesus in Bethlehem	*Matthew* 1:25
Luke 1:31	Jesus was given his name before his birth	*Matthew* 1:21
Luke 1:32	Jesus was descended from David	*Matthew* 1:1
Luke 2:51	Jesus, Mary and Joseph, sometimes called 'the holy family', finally settled down in Nazareth	*Matthew* 2:23

The Birth of Jesus

Copied or separately written?

There is no convincing evidence that the authors of either *Luke* or *Matthew* copied their nativity stories from each other. Most scholars believe that each evangelist wrote his account separately. Why?

Differences

On comparing the two Gospel accounts, one notices that *Luke* includes details in his account that *Matthew* does not and vice-versa.

- *Luke* 3:23–38 and *Matthew* 1:1–16 each give a different *genealogy* (i.e. family tree) for Jesus. *Luke* traces Jesus' family line all the way back to Adam, the name traditionally given to the first human being, while *Matthew* traces his line back to Abraham, the father of the Jewish people.

- Whereas *Luke* (1:26–38) tells us the story of how the angel Gabriel appeared to Mary (i.e. the annunciation), *Matthew* (1:18–25) tells us how an angel spoke to Joseph in a dream.

- *Luke*'s version of the nativity has shepherds visiting the baby Jesus (*Luke* 2:8–20), but he never mentions the Magi (the wise men).

However, while *Matthew* does mention the story of the Magi (*Matthew* 2:1–12), he makes no mention of the shepherds.

The Annunciation by El Greco (16th Century).

All About Faith

Common Purpose

It is very easy to get caught up in the details of the Christmas story. But if we do so we can miss the important truths that the evangelists were trying to communicate:

- *Luke* wanted his readers to know that Jesus came to bring God's love and forgiveness to people of all social classes, whether they were poor shepherds or wealthy nobles.
- *Matthew* used the story of the Magi to drive home the point that Jesus had come into the world to show the power of God's love, not just to the Jews, but to <u>all</u> humankind.

Although *Luke* and *Matthew* offer different accounts of Jesus' birth, they agree on many details and, more importantly, on the <u>meaning</u> of his birth.

They show Jesus to be the fulfilment of all human hopes and the greatest sign of God's love for everyone.

QUESTIONS

(1) On what points of the nativity story do *Luke* and *Matthew* agree?

(2) Why do most scholars believe that each evangelist wrote his account separately? Give reasons for your answer.

(3) Explain the following: (a) <u>genealogy</u>, (b) <u>annunciation</u>.

(4) Behind the differences in their accounts of the nativity, what important messages did *Luke* and *Matthew* want to get across to their readers about the birth of Jesus?

CHAPTER TEN

A PORTRAIT OF JESUS

Appearance

The *New Testament* does not offer us a physical description of Jesus, nor has any painting or sculpture of Jesus been found that dates from the first century A.D. The early Christians do not seem to have been interested in what Jesus looked like. Why?

The main reason for this may have been that most of Jesus' early followers were Jews. According to the Jewish religion, any attempt to produce an image of either God or a human being was wrong and was condemned as an offence against God's law.

The Jews believed all paintings and sculptures to be 'graven images' that would only lead people away from the worship of God. Similarly, they also considered any written descriptions to be just as disrespectful and avoided them too.

Another reason may have been the <u>intention</u> of the *New Testament* writers. For them, the important thing was not how Jesus looked but <u>who he is</u> and <u>what he did</u>. They wrote the *New Testament* to explain the meaning and importance of Jesus' words and deeds for the people of their own time.

Can we say anything therefore about Jesus' appearance? Yes, though only by piecing together a number of clues <u>unintentionally</u> scattered throughout the Gospels.

For example:

- Jesus was a carpenter by profession. He was used to working out of doors in extreme weather conditions. As such his skin would have been leathered and heavily tanned by the sun. He would, in all likelihood, have had a muscular build and if you had shook hands with him you would probably have noticed how calloused his hands were.
- The Gospels tell us that Jesus was well-used to walking long distances, that he spent entire nights deep in prayer and that he fasted for long periods.

This suggests that Jesus was physically healthy and strong. Whether Jesus was physically attractive and noble in appearance, as some artists have portrayed him, we cannot say.

His personality

The Gospels offer us important insights into the personality of Jesus.

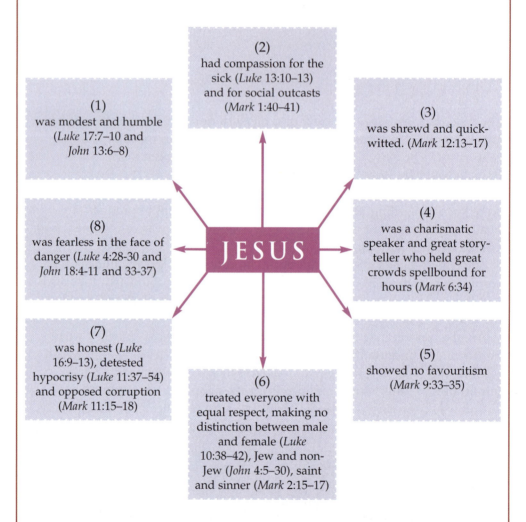

(1) was modest and humble (*Luke* 17:7–10 and *John* 13:6–8)

(2) had compassion for the sick (*Luke* 13:10–13) and for social outcasts (*Mark* 1:40–41)

(3) was shrewd and quick-witted. (*Mark* 12:13–17)

(4) was a charismatic speaker and great story-teller who held great crowds spellbound for hours (*Mark* 6:34)

(5) showed no favouritism (*Mark* 9:33–35)

(6) treated everyone with equal respect, making no distinction between male and female (*Luke* 10:38–42), Jew and non-Jew (*John* 4:5–30), saint and sinner (*Mark* 2:15–17)

(7) was honest (*Luke* 16:9–13), detested hypocrisy (*Luke* 11:37–54) and opposed corruption (*Mark* 11:15–18)

(8) was fearless in the face of danger (*Luke* 4:28-30 and *John* 18:4-11 and 33-37)

N.B. It is clear that Jesus had a uniquely warm and highly attractive personality. Little wonder that many of those who encountered him developed a deep and lasting love for him (*John* 11:1–6).

A Portrait of Jesus

QUESTIONS

(1) Do we possess any physical description of Jesus dating from the first century A.D.?

(2) What did Jews in the time of Jesus believe about paintings and sculptures of people?

(3) What was the Jewish attitude to written descriptions of a person?

(4) Why were early Christians not interested in recording the details of Jesus' physical appearance?

(5) Do the Gospels provide us with any clues about Jesus' physical appearance? If so, what can we say?

(6) In your own words, write your own portrait of Jesus' personality. Consult your copy of the *New Testament*.

(7) Why do many scholars believe that Jesus had a warm and highly attractive personality? Explain your answer.

Images of Jesus

Over the centuries, painters have produced many different images of Jesus. Each of these paintings portrays an <u>aspect</u> of Jesus' personality or his mission on earth that had a particular appeal to people during the artist's life-time.

▲ Catacombs, Rome.
Source: M. Gough, Origins of Christian Art.
Thames and Hudson.

Ancient
[Jesus the Good Shepherd]

The early Christians suffered repeated persecution and this painting shows how they believed that Jesus cares for those who remain faithful to him and will grant them everlasting life.

Medieval
[Jesus the Pantocrator (Ruler of the Universe)]

▲ Mosaics of either San Vitale or Ravenna.

The nations of Europe were ruled over by kings who expected their people to be loyal and pledge their lives to them. Christians accepted this type of government but believed that Jesus was the 'King of kings' to whom everyone, whether king or ordinary person, had to look up to and worship.

Renaissance
[Jesus the Judge of All]

Christians were very aware of how short life can be after the terrible years of the Black Death. They thought a great deal about life after death and how a person might enjoy eternal life in heaven and avoid hell.

▲ Michelangelo's Last Judgement, Sistine Chapel, Rome.

Modern
[Jesus the Suffering Saviour]

▲ Grunewald's Christ on the Cross.

In modern times Christians have taken greater notice of their belief that <u>Jesus is both God and a human being</u>. Some artists have tried to show that Jesus understands the suffering life can bring and that he is with us even in the worst of times.

A Portrait of Jesus

It is unlikely that any of these painters show Jesus as he actually appeared. However, each of these different artworks helps us to understand something of Jesus' mission and his continuing importance for Christians throughout history.

QUESTIONS

(1) Which of the four images of Jesus above is your favourite? Explain your choice.

(2) Draw your own image of Jesus. Then write a brief note explaining the meaning of your image.

CHAPTER ELEVEN

LIFE IN PALESTINE

Introduction

When Jesus spoke to the people who gathered to hear him teach, he told them stories using images and events drawn from their everyday home life and work experience to get his message across.

Communities

In the time of Jesus, the people of Palestine lived in one or other of the following types of community:

- the long established Jewish cities and towns such as Jerusalem, Bethlehem and Nazareth
- the more recent Roman-built urban centres such as Caesarea and Tiberias
- the small rural farming communities dotted across the more arable areas of the region.

Political regions

In the first century A.D., the principal political regions of Palestine were Galilee in the north, Samaria in the centre and Judaea in the south. When Jesus was born all three regions had been united for many years under the rule of King Herod the Great. Herod was allowed rule the area on behalf of Rome but only as long as he kept it peaceful and collected taxes for the emperor.

After Herod's death, his sons proved poor administrators. So the emperor appointed a Roman official to act as *procurator* (i.e. governor) of Samaria and Judaea. One of Herod's sons, Herod Antipater, was allowed to rule over what the Romans considered to be the least important area of Palestine — Galilee.

Although Jesus was born in Bethlehem in Judaea, he grew up in the old Jewish town of Nazareth in Galilee.

Life in Palestine

▲ Palestine's political regions.

QUESTIONS

(1) What were the three types of community in Palestine?

(2) What were its three principal political regions?

(3) Why, do you think, the Romans let Herod the Great rule Palestine?

(4) Why did the emperor later appoint a procurator to administer Samaria and Judaea?

(5) Where did Jesus grow up?

(6) Why, do you think, did Jesus teach with stories that used images and events drawn from people's everyday lives in Palestine?

Work

Despite all the great political upheavals caused by successive waves of invaders and occupiers which struck Palestine over the centuries, the life of most ordinary people remained relatively unchanged whether their rulers were Persians, Greeks or Romans. Most Jews found employment in one or other of the following categories of manual work:

- Farming
- Fishing
- Craft-work

▲ Israel. Shepherd and sheep in the Golan Heights.

Farming

The average Jewish farmer did not live on his farm but in a village nearby where he had access to a water supply. Large farmers employed workers to shepherd their goats and sheep, grow cereal crops, work in their orchards of fig and olive trees, or to tend to the vines that produced grapes for wine. Smaller farmers tended to specialise in one area and usually employed only family members to cut costs.

Though Palestine had been called the 'promised land', a large part of its landscape was rock and sand, unsuited to agriculture. Even in its more arable areas farmers had to contend with such challenges as:

- Drought
- The sirocco, i.e. strong winds from the east that could strip away the dry top soil
- Plagues of locusts which would devour crops.

Farmers and their workers generally endured lives of back-breaking toil and hardship.

Fishing

Most fishermen worked in family groups, living in the towns and villages dotted around the Sea of Galilee, an inland freshwater lake about twelve miles long and six miles wide through which the river Jordan flows. Fish was an important source of food as it could be cooked and eaten fresh or dried and salted, to be eaten later.

Jesus chose his first disciples from the fishing communities around the Sea of Galilee. It is thought that at least seven of the twelve apostles were fishermen.

Craft work

Jewish writings from the first century mention such crafts as:

- Baking
- Carpentry
- Pottery
- Sandal-making
- Ship-building
- Tailoring
- Tent-making

There were trade guilds and each guild had its own small section in larger urban settlements. Craftsmen were generally held in high regard. Most educated men also learned a trade to ensure they could earn a living, e.g. Jesus himself was a carpenter.

▲ Israel. Fisherman carrying his nets.

QUESTIONS

(1) State the three categories of manual work in which most Jews found employment.

(2) Why did most farmers live in villages?

(3) What were the challenges faced by all farmers?

(4) Where did most fishing take place?

(5) Why was fish an important source of food?

(6) Describe the position of a craftsman in Jewish society.

The professional class

In addition to those who earned their living by physical labour, there was a relatively small group of educated people who did not do manual work but instead earned their living as administrators, doctors and merchant traders. Among the most influential were the *scribes*, i.e. professional copyists and religious teachers who were addressed as <u>rabbi</u> (meaning: 'my master').

Tax collectors

Tax collectors were despised by most of their fellow Jews. The Romans sold the right to collect taxes to certain Jews who then acted as collection agents for the region's Roman procurator.

Most Jews earned just enough to provide for the basic necessities of life: food, clothing and shelter. Few were wealthy. Yet the Romans imposed heavy taxes which, though they bitterly resented them, the Jews dared not refuse to pay.

Those Jews who supervised and carried out the collection of these unfair taxes were considered <u>traitors</u>. Further, because some of these tax collectors kept a proportion of the money they collected for themselves, they were denounced as <u>thieves</u>.

Most Jews treated tax collectors as social outcasts. Tax collectors were disqualified from holding any religious office and were not allowed to give evidence in a Jewish court, because they were considered cheats and liars.

Jesus horrified many of his followers and angered his critics when he even held a conversation with a tax collector. Imagine, then, the reaction there must have been when Jesus invited one named Matthew to become one of his close circle of friends.

▲ Tax collector.

QUESTIONS

(1) What was the 'professional class'?

(2) What was a <u>scribe</u>?

(3) Why did most Jews resent paying taxes to the Romans?

(4) What did most Jews think of those who collected these taxes?

(5) Is it true to say that tax collectors were treated as social outcasts? Give reasons for your answer.

(6) Which of the apostles was once a tax collector?

CHAPTER TWELVE

GROWING UP IN NAZARETH

Location

▲ Nazareth today.

Jesus grew up in the province of Galilee in northern Palestine. The region is hilly and mountainous, especially the further north you travel. Its highest point is Mount Meiron which rises to 3,963 feet above sea level.

Jesus spent most of his childhood and early adult life in Nazareth, a town in southern Galilee. At 1,230 feet above sea level, Nazareth was situated in the hills overlooking the Plain of Esdraelon.

Today Nazareth is a large, thriving urban centre with a population of about 60,000 people. However, 2000 years ago, it was just a small village built around a spring well. Nazareth was close to a number of important trade routes so, while it was somewhat out of the way by our standards it was not completely remote. Indeed, its inhabitants traded with other towns and villages which, although heavily populated by their fellow Jews, also included Arabs, Greeks, Phoenicians and Syrians too.

Sources

The Gospels tell us very little about either the childhood or early adulthood of Jesus. Neither <u>Mark's</u> nor <u>John's</u> Gospels say anything whatsoever about what Jesus said and did before he began his public ministry of teaching and healing at about the age of thirty. Although the Gospels of *Matthew* and *Luke* tell the story of the events surrounding the birth of Jesus, only *Luke* makes any mention of an event between Jesus' birth and the time in which he began his public ministry about thirty years later. (see *Luke* 2:41–52).

The evangelists were more interested in recording the events of those last three years of Jesus' life on earth because they revealed him to be the Messiah whom they had hoped God would send.

Jesus as a boy working in Joseph's carpentry shop.
▼

All About Faith

QUESTIONS

(1) Where is Nazareth situated?

(2) Which Gospels offer us any information about Jesus' early life?

(3) Why were the four Gospel writers more interested in the years of Jesus' public ministry?

Cut-away drawing of a Jewish home.
▼

- While the well-to-do minority lived in comfortable Roman-style houses (villas), the average house in a town like Nazareth was white-washed both inside and outside. There were no bathing facilities inside.
- Fixed to the right-hand doorpost at the entrance to the house was a little wooden or leather case called a 'Mazuzah'. It contained a tiny scroll with the words of the 'Shema', a prayer taken from the Old Testament book of Deuteronomy, 6:4. A devout Jew would always touch the Mazuzah before entering and when leaving his/her home.
- The family slept upstairs. Most family members slept on mats which were rolled up and stored when not in use.
- The lower level was used at night as a stable to keep the family's animals safe. The family members themselves lived on a raised platform of beaten earth covered with straw. Sometimes stone chippings were pressed into the earth to form a floor.
- As there were no windows, the interior was cool but dark, as there was no natural light. So an oil lamp was always kept burning in a little alcove in the family's upper living area to provide light.
- At meal times the family sat cross-legged on the floor around a circular mat or low table on which their food was placed. They were not served individual portions. Instead they shared a common bowl, dipping in and taking their food with their right hands.
- The house had a flat roof made from mud-caked reed mats which were spread over and secured to rows of parallel wooden beams which supported the roof. When it rained heavily and for a long period of time, such a roof was liable to severe leaking.
- There was no real fireplace as such. A fire was kept lit in a shallow pit in the floor or in a large earthenware pot. Charcoal, thorns and dried animal dung were used to fuel the fire. There was no chimney, so during the colder winter months, the house was often filled with smoke. In summer the smoke from the fire helped ward off insects.
- There was very little furniture, perhaps a few stools. Utensils were usually stored in little alcoves in the wall. Wine skins were hung from hooks on the roof beams. Water drawn from the local well was stored in porous earthenware jars in which the water remained cool by a process of slow evaporation.

Diet: This consisted of goat's cheese, eggs, porridge, beans, lentils, cucumber, dates, figs and pomegranates. Those living near waterways ate fish. Watered-down wine was served at meal times, as was goat's milk.

Attitudes to children

The Jews considered children to be a blessing and gift from God (see *Psalm* 127). Children were seen as the hope for a better future and as the inheritors of the covenant (i.e. sacred agreement) which God had made with Abraham. Generally, however, fathers tended to place greater value on a male child because he was expected to carry on the family name and, by inheriting all his father's property, keep it in the family. Women were treated as second-class citizens, something which Jesus would later oppose strongly.

▲ Michelangelo's Holy family with St John (16th Century).

Naming

When a baby boy was eight days old he was formally named at a ceremony in the local *synagogue* (i.e. community house of prayer). The name chosen always had a meaning. It usually said something about what kind of person his parents hoped he would grow up to be, or expressed how the family felt about God. For example the Old Testament prophet Isaiah's name means 'God is salvation'. The name Jesus is derived from the Old Testament hero Joshua meaning 'saviour'. According to *Matthew* 1:21, Jesus received this name because his foster father Joseph had been told to do so by an angel. The choice of a child's name was usually decided by the father, although the mother would sometimes be consulted.

▲ Ioannina Synagogue in Jerusalem.

Circumcision

On the same day as he was named, Jesus would have been *circumcised*, i.e. the top part of the loose foreskin over his penis would have been cut off. The Jews believed that had been demanded of them by God when he made the covenant with Abraham (see *Genesis* 17:9–14). It served to:

- mark physically all Jewish males as members of God's chosen people and
- remind them always to treat each other with justice and compassion.

Education

Jesus would have attended school at the local synagogue between the ages of seven and thirteen. In addition to reading, writing and basic maths, he would have been expected to memorise and then recite long extracts from the Jewish scriptures (i.e. *Old Testament*). This would have been very demanding as these texts were written in Hebrew, the ancient language of the Jews, rather than Aramaic, the language spoken by most Jews in Palestine at that time.

Becoming an adult

When Jesus reached the age of thirteen he would have gone to the local synagogue to have his religious knowledge publicly examined by the rabbi.

In front of all the local adult males, Jesus would have been questioned to establish whether or not he was well versed in the *Torah*, i.e. <u>laws guiding how a Jew should live as set out in the first five books of the Bible</u>. When he passed this he would have been declared *Bar Mitzvah* (meaning: 'son of the law'). He was then said to have 'come of age' and was recognised as a man.

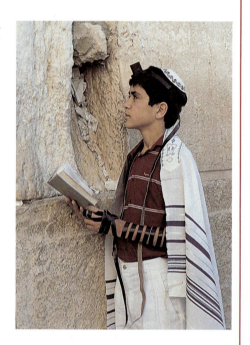

▲ Jerusalem, Barmitzvah boy praying.

QUESTIONS

(1) What was the Jewish attitude to children?

(2) Why did the father usually place a greater value on a male child?

(3) How did Jewish parents approach the task of naming a child?

(4) What does the name 'Jesus' mean?

(5) What is *circumcision*?

(6) Why are all Jewish males circumcised?

(7) What is the *Torah*?

(8) Explain the <u>meaning</u> and <u>importance</u> of *Bar Mitzvah* for the Jews

CHAPTER THIRTEEN

UNDER ROMAN RULE

Pontius Pilate

In the summer of A.D. 26, the newly appointed Roman procurator (i.e. governor) of the provinces of Judaea and Samaria stepped ashore at the great sea port of Caesarea. His name was Pontius Pilate. His mission was:

- to ensure that the local population paid their taxes promptly to the emperor and
- to keep the area peaceful and the trade routes open.

Making an impression

For anyone observing the large display of Roman troops which greeted Pilate's arrival at Caesarea, there could be no doubting the power of the empire.

The rows of men in shining armour looked very impressive. Their fearsome reputation seemed justified. Didn't everyone know that the Roman army had easily conquered Palestine?

What everyone did <u>not</u> know was that the Roman garrison at Pilate's disposal was never more than three thousand men. The nearest reinforcements were hundreds of miles away in either Egypt or Syria.

The key to Roman power in Palestine and throughout their empire was twofold:

- The threat of force
  Pilate had to keep almost three quarters of a million people convinced that it was

Roman soldiers on the march.

pointless trying to oppose Roman rule. A large network of informants was set up throughout Palestine, and these helped the Roman authorities to quickly identify and eliminate anyone who might pose a threat and so discourage any ideas of rebellion.

- Ruling by co-operation

The Romans recognised the importance of having the co-operation of influential figures from among the peoples they had conquered. If Pilate wanted to administer his province in the smooth and efficient way the emperor demanded, he needed the help of the most influential Jews in Palestine. There were a number of Jews who were quite willing to do so.

QUESTIONS

(1) What was Pontius Pilate's mission as governor?

(2) What was the key to Roman power? Explain how it worked.

The Sanhedrin

No matter what Pilate or any other Roman said, even the most co-operative Jews believed that God not the emperor really ruled their people. Realising how their religion played such a central role in Jewish life, the Romans demanded and received the loyal support of the Jewish Sanhedrin in governing Palestine.

The Sanhedrin served as both
- the ruling council of the Jewish religion and
- its highest law court.

The 'Sadducee' and the 'Zealot'.

The Jews of the Sanhedrin were divided, however, by two key questions:
 (1) How they should interpret and apply their religious laws to everyday life, and
 (2) How Jewish people should relate to and treat non-Jews.

Basically the Sanhedrin's members formed into two rival groups on these issues:
- the Sadducees and
- the Pharisees

Each claimed to uphold the true ideals of the Jewish religion.

These two groups combined to form a council of seventy elders, from among whom a high priest was elected to direct the Sanhedrin's activities. The Romans allowed the Sanhedrin to:
- serve as a court of law for the Jewish population
- have its own temple guards to keep order
- punish Jews who broke the laws of their own religion.

However, the Sanhedrin was <u>not</u> allowed to impose the death penalty.

Although Pilate never let the Jews forget that they were subjects of the emperor, the Jews were permitted a considerable degree of self-rule. As we shall see, different groups reacted to this in different ways.

QUESTIONS

(1) What was the Sanhedrin?
(2) What were the two main issues which divided the Sanhedrin's members?
(3) Name its two rival groupings.
(4) Who directed the Sanhedrin's various activities?
(5) Describe the power of the Sanhedrin.

All About Faith

Reactions to Roman rule

The sometimes harsh rule of foreign occupiers, such as the Romans led the Jews to react in different ways and this produced a number of influential groups.

1. Accept Roman rule, adapt to it and make an unwritten agreement to use your influence to keep order.

2. Reject Roman rule and devote all your energy to practising your religion.

THE SADDUCEES

- They were wealthy aristocrats and included the temple priests.
- Dominated the Sanhedrin and controlled the key office of High Priest.
- Adopted non-Jewish life-styles.
- Only accepted the written <u>Torah</u> on religious matters. Interpreted it rigidly and literally. Refused to accept any development of new ideas. Rejected belief in angels and life after death.
- Did not expect a Messiah to deliver them from Roman rule.

THE PHARISEES

- They were laymen not priests. Included the scribes (i.e. teachers of the law) who expected to be called 'rabbi'.
- Controlled local synagogues.
- Name means the <u>separated</u>. Were dedicated to preserving the purity of the Jewish religion but tended to keep themselves apart from ordinary Jews who were not so devout.
- Accepted oral tradition (collected sayings) as well as guidance of the *Torah*. Open to development of new religious ideas. Believed in angels and life after death.
- Expected a Messiah to free them from Roman rule and establish a kingdom as in the days of King David.

3. Reject Roman rule, opt out of society altogether and set up religious communities in remote desert areas.

4. Reject Roman rule and form a resistance movement to violently oppose it.

THE ESSENES

- They were communities of monks who settled in remote places. Believed they were obeying the word of God (see *Isaiah* 40:3).
- Thought to have set up community at Qumran where the *Dead Sea Scrolls* were found.
- Felt that Jewish religion was being corrupted by outside influences. Believed that they alone had the correct interpretation of the *Torah*.
- Followed strict rule of life. Three year training period. New members had to swear to keep their teachings and practices secret.
- Placed great emphasis on bathing. May have influenced John the Baptist.

THE ZEALOTS

- They were deeply religious Jews who believed violent action was justified if it was in defence of the Jewish religion.
- Possibly an off-shoot of the Pharisees.
- Hated the Sadducees for working with the Romans. One group of the Zealots known as the Sicarii (cut-throats) engaged in a campaign of assassination.
- Caused a great deal of unrest among the people. Jesus was viewed with suspicion for having a Zealot (Simon the Patriot) among his apostles.

QUESTIONS

(1) Explain briefly the reaction of each of the following to Roman rule of Palestine:
- The Sadducees
- The Pharisees
- The Essenes
- The Zealots

(2) Which group dominated the Sanhedrin and controlled the key office of High Priest?

(3) What is the meaning of the title 'Pharisee'?

(4) State two differences between the Sadducees and the Pharisees.

(5) What was the name given to the communities of Jewish monks who settled in remote areas such as Qumran?

(6) Which group believed that violent action was justified in defence of the Jewish religion? Which of the apostles belonged to this group?

CHAPTER FOURTEEN

JOHN THE BAPTIST

A new Elijah

Most Jews believed that, before the Messiah would appear, the *Old Testament* prophet Elijah would return from heaven to announce his arrival (Read *John* 1:21 and 1:25). Elijah (name means: *My God is Yahweh*) was a Jewish holy man or prophet who lived in the ninth century B.C. He was a fearless preacher, an ascetic (i.e. someone who lived a life of self-denial) who urged the Jews of his time to worship the God of Abraham and Moses, who defended the poor and powerless, and openly opposed corruption.

The Gospels of *Luke* and *John* both present John the Baptist as a new Elijah. John, whose name means *God has been gracious*, was the son of Zechariah, a temple priest, and Elizabeth, a cousin of Jesus' mother Mary. The story of John's birth is told in *Luke* 1:5–25 and 1:57–80. John is clearly identified as the herald of the Messiah, i.e. the one who forewarns the people and prepares them for his arrival. (see *Luke* 1:17).

The herald of the Messiah

Using the information contained in *Luke* 3:1–2, it seems that John the Baptist began his public preaching and baptising around A.D. 28–29. The four Gospels portray John the Baptist as a rather fearsome and outspoken individual. He wore only a rough garment made from camel hair, with a leather loin cloth around his waist. He lived in hostile desert areas and survived by eating only locusts and wild honey (*Matthew* 3:4 and *Mark* 1:6).

John's symbol in Christian art is the Lion. It reminds Christians that he was the one whom *Isaiah* 40:3 descried as 'a voice calling in the wilderness'.

← Israel. The Judean wilderness on the west coast of the Dead Sea.

John's message

John the Baptist was a man in a great hurry. He did not use gentle words to win people over. He was blunt and forthright in his statements. For example, he denounced the Pharisees and the Sadducees, calling them a *'brood of vipers'* (*Matthew* 3:7–10).

John believed that human beings were so weakened by sin that the only hope for the future was with God. John preached that all of history was coming to a great moment of change, when a whole new age of peace and justice would begin.

John said that at last God had sent the Messiah and that it was his task to prepare the people for his coming. John urged them *to repent* (i.e. show sorrow for their sins) and *be baptised*. This baptism involved each person being completely immersed in the River Jordan as a sign that their sins had been washed away by God's forgiveness.

▲ Upper Galilee. Aerial view of River Jordan.

John called on people, both Jews and non-Jews, to share with those in need, treat people honestly and accept a fair wage (read *Luke* 3:10–14). He denied that he was the Messiah (*John* 1:20). He told the crowds around him that the Messiah was one who already stood among them, one whose sandals he was not worthy to untie. [In that time, removing a guest's shoes was a task performed by a lowly servant]. John told people that whereas he baptised them with water, the Messiah would pour out the wonderful gift of God's Holy Spirit upon them.

The death of John the Baptist

John, like Elijah before him, was not afraid of challenging powerful and dangerous people. He criticised Herod Antipas, ruler of Galilee, for marrying Herodias. He said that Herod's action was wrong because Herodias had been the wife of Herod's brother Philip who was still alive. Herod had John imprisoned and executed.

QUESTIONS

(1) Who was Elijah?

(2) What did many Jews believe about Elijah?

(3) What is an ascetic?

(4) What did John's name mean?

(5) Why is John the Baptist called the herald of the Messiah?

(6) Why did John baptise people with water?

(7) Why was John the Baptist executed?

(8) Read the text above once more. Then write a brief essay on John the Baptist, describing the kind of person he was.

CHAPTER FIFTEEN

THE BAPTISM OF JESUS

According to *Matthew* 3:13–15, Jesus went to John the Baptist and asked to be baptised like everyone else in the waters of the river Jordan. John the Baptist was very reluctant to do this because he realised that Jesus was the promised Messiah. John did not feel worthy and asked Jesus to baptise him instead. Jesus gently insisted with his request, however, so John relented and baptised him.

The Gospels tell us that when Jesus was baptised the *Holy Spirit* descended on Jesus in the form of a <u>dove</u> (this was meant to represent the peaceful presence of God) and that a voice spoke to Jesus from heaven. This may have been experienced only by Jesus (see *Matthew*, *Mark* and *Luke*) or it may have been witnessed by others too (*John* 1:32–34).

The puzzle of Jesus' baptism

When he baptised people in the river Jordan, John the Baptist was reminding them that, because they had repented, their sins had been forgiven. God was offering each of them a fresh start and a chance to prepare for the coming of the Messiah.

The early Christians found the story of Jesus' baptism very puzzling. They believed that Jesus was the Son of God. He was perfect and had never committed a single sin. So why did the sinless Son of God ask John to baptise him

Baptism of Christ by Della Francesca (15th Century). ➡

when he did <u>not</u> need to say sorry for anything?

Only *Matthew* 3:15 offers an answer to this question.

By being baptised, Jesus was not admitting that he had ever sinned. Rather, Jesus was showing how he wanted to completely identify himself with the lives and daily struggles of the people. Jesus would share in all the joys and sorrows of those around him. He was ready to *do all that righteousness demanded*, even if it eventually meant his death on a cross (see also *Mark* 10:38 and *Luke* 12:50).

▲ Baptism of Jesus in the Jordan.

The importance of Jesus' baptism

The baptism story is more than just an account of how Jesus received his baptism from John the Baptist. It is also the story of how, through the power of the Holy Spirit, Jesus came to understand who he was and what God, <u>his Father</u>, was calling him to do.

Jesus realised that he had a unique mission to fulfil. He would reveal through his words and actions the awesome power of God's love and forgiveness.

QUESTIONS

(1) Why was John the Baptist unwilling at first to baptise Jesus?

(2) What do the Gospels say happened when Jesus was baptised?

(3) Was Jesus the only person to have witnessed the Holy Spirit descending as a dove and to have heard the voice of God the Father?

(4) Why did John baptise people?

(5) Why did the early Christians find the story of Jesus' baptism puzzling at first?

(6) What explanation did *Matthew* offer for Jesus' baptism?

(7) What do you think that the phrase *doing all that righteousness demanded* means?

(8) When Jesus was baptised he came to understand what his mission in life was. In your own words, explain what that was.

CHAPTER SIXTEEN

THE TEMPTATIONS IN THE DESERT

Sources

After Jesus' baptism, *Mark* 1:12–13 briefly states that

> '*the Holy Spirit led him out into the wilderness and he remained there for forty days and was tempted by Satan.*'

While *John* does not refer to this incident at all, both *Luke* and *Matthew* do. Probably drawing on information contained in the Q document, *Luke* 4:1–13 and *Matthew* 4:1–11 offer more detailed accounts. Although their accounts differ slightly on the order in which the events took place, both *Luke* and *Matthew* agree on content.

Purpose

The story of Jesus fasting and praying alone in the Judaean wilderness is full of references to events and sayings drawn from the *Old Testament*.

▼ Israel. The Monastery of the Temptation above Jericho.

- Like Moses before him, Jesus needed to prepare for his mission to lead God's people (see *Exodus* 34:28). Jesus needed to pray about the kind of Messiah he would be.

- When the Jewish people escaped from slavery in Egypt they spent forty years in the wilderness where they faced many temptations. But, while they had on occasion given into temptation, Jesus never did. He remained faithful to God the Father. According to *Luke*, Jesus was tempted in three ways. In response to each temptation, Jesus quoted words of wisdom from the *Old Testament* book of *Deuteronomy*.

- Jesus was tempted to use his power for himself by turning stones into bread (*Luke* 4:3). Jesus knew, however, that while food is a basic necessity, people need more than just food to live a truly human existence, and quoted *Deuteronomy* 8:3 at Satan: <u>Man cannot live on bread alone</u>.
- Then Jesus was tempted to turn his back on his mission and worship Satan instead. In return for doing this, Satan would give Jesus all the wealth and power necessary to make people follow and obey him. Jesus rejected any idea that the Messiah would be a warrior leader who would set up some new, rich earthly empire in place of Rome. He recalled *Deuteronomy* 6:13 in response: <u>You must worship the Lord your God and serve him alone</u>.
- Finally Jesus was tempted to use his power to impress people by throwing himself from the highest point of the temple (a 450 foot drop) and have God send his angels to save him. Jesus saw no value whatsoever in such a dramatic gesture. God's power would not be revealed through stupid stunts designed to win over people. Jesus quoted *Deuteronomy* 6:16 at Satan: <u>You must not put the Lord your God to the test</u>.

The continuing struggle

Luke tells us that once Satan realised that he had failed to sway Jesus from his mission, he left Jesus alone. However, *Luke* ends saying that Satan would <u>return at the appointed time</u> (*Luke* 4:13).

Jesus would have to face these temptations again and again during his ministry. Jesus realised that the path which lay before him would involve his suffering, rejection and death.

QUESTIONS

(1) Which Gospels offer the <u>fullest</u> account of the temptations of Jesus?

(2) In what ways did the story of Jesus' temptations make references to events in the *Old Testament*?

(3) From which *Old Testament* book did Jesus draw wise words of guidance when tempted by Satan?

(4) State each of the temptations. Then, in your own words, explain why Jesus resisted each of them in turn.

CHAPTER SEVENTEEN

JESUS BEGINS HIS PUBLIC MINISTRY

Introduction

After his experiences in the Judaean desert, Jesus returned to Galilee, where he began his ministry of healing and preaching. Following his rejection by his former neighbours in Nazareth (*Matthew* 13:53–58 and *Luke* 4:16–30) Jesus moved to Capernaum on the shores of the Sea of Galilee. There he began to draw large crowds as word spread about the extraordinary things he taught and did.

Originality

Throughout his preaching, Jesus made use of the Jewish Scriptures (what Christians call the *Old Testament*). Jesus' words had a profound effect on many of those who heard him preach. Perhaps because they realised that Jesus always practised what he preached.

Jesus preaching.

> 'His teaching made a deep impression on the people because he taught them with authority, and not like their own scribes'. (*Matthew* 7:28–29).

Yet Jesus did not actually teach anything that could not be found in the Jewish scriptures as such. He was not original in the sense of creating a whole new set of moral rules by which people should live.

Where Jesus was original, however, was the way in which he made new connections in the ancient teachings of his people. For example, Jesus linked two separate *Old Testament* texts *Deuteronomy* 6:5 and *Leviticus* 19:18 in a way no one else had before. He used them to form the very heart of his message:

That we should love God with all our heart and our neighbours as

Jesus Begins His Public Ministry

ourselves.

Jesus took existing religious ideas in Judaism and explained them in a new and refreshing way. He sought to help people to see the <u>deeper meanings</u> that had always rested within their ancient writings.

> *'Do not imagine that I have come to abolish the Torah or the Prophets. I have come not to abolish but to complete them.'*
> *(Matthew 5:17)*

Sometimes, however, Jesus <u>was</u> strikingly original and rejected certain teachings that had become accepted among his fellow Jews. By the first century A.D. all Jews were expected to follow 613 laws which covered every aspect of a person's life. For example, according to Jewish law, a person was not allowed to whisk away a fly that had landed on his body during the Sabbath day. He/She simply had to wait until the fly decided to go away. A devout Jew was expected to know every law and follow it without exception. If he/she did not, then it was believed that person would be punished by God.

Jesus saw how all this *legalism* (i.e. harsh and excessive devotion to the precise letter of the law) had become a terrible burden for so many good people. Jesus offered an alternative to this (see *Matthew* 11:25–30). His teaching was challenging but <u>life-giving</u>, emphasising <u>love of God</u> rather than fear of God.

Jesus publicly confronted the Pharisees who promoted such legalism. For example, he taught that the law which required everyone to rest on the Sabbath day on pain of death (see *Numbers* 15:32–36) could be broken. He did so himself when he healed a sick person (see *Luke* 6:6–11). Some rules were more important than others.

As we shall see later, Jesus' preaching shocked and angered powerful religious groups such as the Pharisees, who considered themselves to be the only people fit to preach about God's laws.

QUESTIONS

(1) Why did Jesus move to Capernaum?
(2) Read *Matthew* 7:28–29. What point does the evangelist make about Jesus?
(3) How did Jesus interpret the ancient Jewish scriptures in a new way?
(4) What is *legalism*? Give an example.
(5) Why did Jesus oppose legalism?
(6) Who did Jesus anger and offend by his preaching? Why did they react in this way?

CHAPTER EIGHTEEN

THE DISCIPLES

Becoming a disciple

▲ Jesus gathering the disciples.

A reader of the Gospels will quickly realise that Jesus enjoyed the company of people and made many friends. However, these people were more than just friends of Jesus, they were also his disciples [from the Latin *discipulus* meaning a student or learner]. These *disciples* were expected to learn from Jesus and follow his example.

In the ancient world it was normal practice for an intending student to select a rabbi [the Jewish title for a teacher of their religion]. With Jesus and his disciples, however, the relationship was very different:

- The disciples did not choose Jesus, rather he chose them. They responded to his call. Jesus completely captured their attention and won their devotion because he practised what he preached.
- Unlike students then or now, the disciples would never have reached a stage where they would have learned all that their teacher had to offer. They would never 'graduate' from Jesus' school of life, because Jesus always offers something more to learn. Christians believe that Jesus is the source of a wisdom that can never be exhausted.

Examining the stories

Read the following Gospel extracts: *Mark* 1:16–20, *Luke* 5:1–11 and *John* 1: 35–50. Though they differ in detail, each presents its story using the same structure:

- Jesus passes by and sees someone.
- An account is given of that person's work.
- Jesus invites the person to become his disciple.
- The person leaves everything and follows Jesus.

The meaning of discipleship

The Gospels present Jesus' call to become his disciple as a huge step in a person's life. It involves a complete break with the way a person has lived his/her life up until then. It demands a *'metanoia'* [Greek word meaning a complete change of heart]. Read *Mark* 2:13–17 and *Luke* 9:57–60.

When people decide to follow Jesus, they become members of a new family. Anyone who follows God's way, as Jesus did by putting obedience to God first and his own comfort last, is a member of his family (see *Mark* 3:33).

The disciples were to be co-workers of Jesus (see *John* 15:16). They were told that by following Jesus they would have to face many challenges to their faith (see *Mark* 8:34–35). They were encouraged to pray so that God would give them the strength they needed (see *Mark* 9:28–29). Finally, a disciple of Jesus would have to be humble and put the good of others before his/her own (see *Mark* 10:35–45).

The Apostles

Luke 10:1–20 tells of Jesus sending out seventy two disciples in pairs to preach and heal. However, within this wide circle of followers, Jesus had a smaller and closer group of disciples whom Christians call the Apostles, although they are usually referred to in the Gospels as the twelve. Their names are recorded in *Luke* 6:13–16, *Mark* 3:16–19 and *Matthew* 10:2–4. *John* does not mention the twelve, preferring to concentrate on Jesus, and only mentions the names of certain apostles to help him make a particular point about Jesus' mission.

The word apostle comes from the Greek word meaning *to send forth*. Jesus selected them to be his constant companions as he travelled throughout Palestine. He gave them a special task which set them apart from the other disciples. After Jesus ascended into heaven, the apostles were to lead his followers and, in his name, *preach*, *heal* and *baptise* new disciples (see *Matthew* 28:16–20).

Jesus may have chosen exactly twelve apostles because of the meaning this number had for the Jews. At one time there had been twelve tribes of Jews, each descended from the sons of Jacob. Jesus may have wanted to suggest that his twelve apostles would be the foundation for a new people of God. Through them he would invite all people, Jew and gentile, into a new community of believers — Christianity.

The apostles came from a variety of different backgrounds:

- Peter, James and John, the disciples who were closest to Jesus, were fishermen.

Peter

Thaddaeus

John

Judas Iscariot

James, son of Alphaeus

Andrew, the brother of Simon Peter

Philip

James, the brother of John

Levi (Matthew), son of Alphaeus

- Matthew (or as he was sometimes called Levi) had been a tax collector.
- Simon had been a zealot.

Sometimes the apostles did not understand the message Jesus was preaching (*Mark* 4:13). Sometimes they quarrelled among themselves (*Mark* 9:33–35). They deserted Jesus when he needed them most (*Matthew* 26:56). One of them, Peter, publicly denied he had ever known Jesus (*Luke* 22:54–62). Another, Judas, betrayed Jesus to his enemies (*Luke* 22:1–6).

However, in each one of them Jesus saw the potential to do great things. Even when they deserted him, Jesus forgave them. After they experienced Jesus risen from the dead, the apostles justified his trust in them and became outstanding leaders who led heroic lives.

Discipleship today

Christians today believe that Jesus calls each person to become his disciple. Jesus invites people to build a personal, lasting relationship with him and to try to live according to the standards he set.

Thomas

Simon the Zealot

Bartholomew

QUESTIONS

(1) Explain each of the following terms:
- disciple
- rabbi
- apostle
- metanoia

(2) In what ways was Jesus' relationship with his disciples different from that of other rabbis in the ancient world?

(3) Read *Mark* 3:33. What do you think is its message?

(4) Read *John* 15:16, *Mark* 8:34–35, 9:28 and 10:35–45. What do they say that Jesus expects of his disciples?

(5) Name the twelve apostles.

(6) Why did Jesus choose twelve apostles?

(7) What role did he want them to play in the future?

CHAPTER NINETEEN

THE KINGDOM OF GOD

Introduction

One phrase occurs again and again in Jesus' preaching: <u>the Kingdom of God</u>. This idea can be traced back to the *Old Testament* writings, but Jesus put it at the very centre of his teaching.

Difficulties

[1.] The very word *kingdom* conjures up an image of a clearly identifiable area of land, marked out on a map and ruled over by a king or queen. Many Jews in Jesus' time hoped that the Messiah would set up an independent Jewish kingdom.

This was <u>not</u> the kind of kingdom Jesus was talking about (see *Luke* 17:20–21 or *John* 18:36).

[2.] Jesus never offered a precise definition of the Kingdom of God. Instead, he used a number of powerful and puzzling images and stories to illustrate its meaning.

Jesus may have done this for two reasons:

- By using pictures and stories, Jesus forced his listeners to think hard about his message and what it demanded of them. He wanted his followers to be serious-minded and committed people.
- The Kingdom of God is a very deep mystery, i.e. so profound that only God fully understands it. Through prayer and good works, people can gain some insights into what it means, but they can never expect to understand it fully.

All About Faith

The meaning of the Kingdom of God

Through the stories he told, Jesus taught his followers that the Kingdom of God is not a place on a map, but a whole new way of life.

- The Kingdom is *in the future* as an ideal or perfect kingdom of goodness, justice and peace where people realise that they are all God's children and members of one family. Jesus looks forward to its coming in the 'Our Father'.
- The Kingdom is also *in the present* as a new society established by the coming of Jesus. Through the life and teaching of Jesus, the Kingdom of God has already come. It exists wherever God's love reigns in people's hearts and where they struggle to live their lives by God's standards.

QUESTIONS

(1) Read *John* 18:36. What point was Jesus making?

(2) Why did Jesus use pictures and stories when talking about the Kingdom of God?

(3) What does it mean to say that the Kingdom of God is a very deep mystery?

(4) If the Kingdom of God is not a place on a map, what then is it?

Israel. The Mount of Beatitudes above the Sea of Galilee. The Franciscan Chapel built in 1937.

Living in the Kingdom

Jesus declared that the Kingdom of God had arrived in him. He called on people to reform their lives in order to enter the Kingdom. Then Jesus taught people how they should live in the Kingdom.

Summaries of this teaching — which were probably given on a number of occasions and in a number of different places — are recorded in *Matthew* chapters 5 to 7 as the Sermon on the Mount and in *Luke* 6:17–49 as the Sermon on the Plain. Both Gospels probably took their common material from *Q*. Both begin with the *Beatitudes*, from the Latin '*beati*' meaning 'happy' or 'blessed'.

The Beatitudes describe the qualities of those people who would be members of the Kingdom of God. *Matthew* talks about:

- **The poor in spirit** These are those who are humble enough to realise that they are weak and selfish and know that they need God's <u>grace</u> (i.e. <u>love and strength</u>) to live good lives.
- **Those that mourn** These people are truly sorry for their own sins and those of all humankind.
- **The meek** Like those mentioned in the first Beatitude, these people have the grace that comes from humility. They are unassuming and do not always stand on their rights. This does not mean that they are weak or liable to be bullied. Their strength and confidence is not in themselves, but in God.
- **Those who hunger and thirst for righteousness** These are those who long for God's rule on earth and desire that his will shall be done in their own lives as well as in society as a whole.
- **The merciful** These are the forgiving.
- **The pure in heart** These people are single-minded in their service of God. Their thoughts are pure and they do not readily attribute evil motives to others.
- **The peacemakers** These are those who yearn and strive for peace in the world and who have peace within themselves because of their trust in God.
- **Those who suffer for righteousness' sake** These endure persecution bravely because of their loyalty to God. They will share the same eternal reward as all the prophets and servants of God who have suffered in the past.

Following the Beatitudes, Jesus continues the Sermon on the Mount and sets out an extraordinarily challenging vision for how his followers should live:

- They should be known for their good works (*Matthew* 5:13–16).
- They should go further than the Jewish law commands. For example, they are to love their enemies (*Matthew* 5:38).
- They should always act with sincerity and without outward show (*Matthew* 6:1–18). Jesus was concerned only with inner goodness.
- They should not condemn others. It is for God to judge others. People should first assess their own behaviour and not live dishonestly with double standards.
- The <u>golden rule</u> should always be their guide: <u>Do unto others as you would have them do unto you</u>. (*Matthew* 7:12).

All About Faith

A genuine follower of Jesus is one who strives to live his/her whole life according to God's standards.

▲ St James of Alcala feeding the poor by Murillo.

QUESTIONS

(1) What does the word <u>beatitude</u> mean?

(2) Where can one find summaries of Jesus' teaching on how people should live in the Kingdom?

(3) Briefly list the qualities possessed by those who strive to be members of God's Kingdom.

(4) What is the <u>golden rule</u>?

(5) Why should Christians not condemn other people?

(6) In what way did Jesus want his followers to go further than the Jewish Law?

CHAPTER TWENTY

THE MIRACLES OF JESUS

Introduction

While John the Baptist was in prison awaiting execution, he heard what Jesus was doing. John had some of his own followers go to Jesus and ask him:

> *'Are you the one who was to come or should we wait for someone else?'*

Jesus answered them:

> *'Go back and report to John what you hear and see: The blind receive sight, the lame walk, those who have leprosy are cured, the deaf hear, the dead are raised and the good news is preached to the poor.'*
> Matthew 11:4–6

The four Gospels record about thirty-five different occasions when Jesus performed a miracle. These miracles were as important to Jesus' ministry as his preaching.

What is a miracle?

The word <u>miracle</u> comes from two Latin words: *'miraculum'* meaning *'a marvel'* and *'mirari'* meaning *'to wonder'*.

A miracle can be broadly defined as:
'a marvellous or wonderful event which occurs as a result of God's direct action.'

The miracles of Jesus fall roughly into four categories:

▲ St Peter's House in Capernaum.

- Healing miracles
- Exorcisms or casting out demons
- Nature miracles
- Restorations of life

Difficulties

For some people the miracle stories create serious problems. They find it hard to believe such things. It is sometimes said that Jesus would be more 'acceptable' without the miracles.

However, it is impossible to extract a miracle-free account of Jesus' ministry from the Gospels for several reasons:

- The whole story of Jesus' conception in Mary's womb is a miracle.
- Much of Jesus' preaching takes a specific miracle as its starting point.
- The miracles are presented as inspiring many of those who witnessed them to have faith in Jesus.
- Christianity itself is founded on the miracle of Jesus' resurrection.

QUESTIONS

(1) Who sent his followers to ask Jesus if he was the long-awaited Messiah?

(2) How many miracles are recorded in the Gospels?

(3) What does the word *miracle* mean?

(4) Name the four types of miracle that Jesus worked.

(5) The following is a list of Jesus' miracles in the Synoptic Gospels

	Matthew	Mark	Luke
Cleansing of a leper	8:1–4	1:40–45	5:12–16
Healing of a centurion's servant	8:5–13		7:1–10
Curing of Peter's mother-in-law	8:14–15	1:29–31	4:38–39
Calming of a storm	8:23–27	4:35–41	8:22–25
Healing of the Gadarene demoniac(s)	8:28–34	5:1–20	8:26–39
Healing of a paralytic	9:1–8	2:1–12	5:17–26
Jairus's daughter and the woman with a haemorrhage	9:18–26	5:21–43	8:40–56
Healing of two blind men	9:27–31		
The man with a withered hand	12:9–14	3:1–6	6:6–11
First miracle of the loaves	14:13–21	6:30–44	9:10–17
Raising of the widow's son			7:11–17
Walking on the water	14:22–33	6:45–52	
Curing of the Canaanite woman's daughter	15:21–28	7:24–30	

The Miracles of Jesus

Healing of a deaf man		7:31–37	
Second miracle of the loaves	15:32–39	8:1–10	
The blind man of Bethsaida		8:22–26	
Healing of a boy with a demon	17:14–20	9:14–29	9:37–42
Cleansing of ten lepers	—	—	17:11–19
Healing blindness at Jericho	20:29–34	10:46–52	18:35–43

Re-organise these miracle stories under the four categories of:
(a) Healing miracles (b) Exorcisms
(c) Restorations of life (d) Nature miracles

(6) Is it possible to extract a miracle-free account of Jesus' ministry from the Gospels?

Did Jesus really work miracles?

Yes. Consider the following points:

- The first century Jewish historian Josephus described Jesus as *a doer of wonderful deeds*.
- Even Jesus' enemies recognised that he had an extraordinary power to work wonders. However, the Pharisees accused Jesus of doing so through the power of the devil (see *Matthew 12:24*).
- Many eyewitnesses to the works of Jesus would still have been alive when the Gospels were written. If the Gospel accounts had not been based on actual events, these people would have raised serious objections to them.

Certain marvellous, miraculous events did happen during the ministry of Jesus. But it is hard for us today to identify or prove in a scientific way exactly what happened during these events.

This difficulty has led some people to think that modern science says that miracles cannot happen. Not so.

- The laws of science describe what it is reasonable for us to expect, i.e. <u>what normally happens</u>.
- However, science does not offer guarantees that things can never be different. Science cannot say that rare and extraordinary events such as miracles cannot happen.

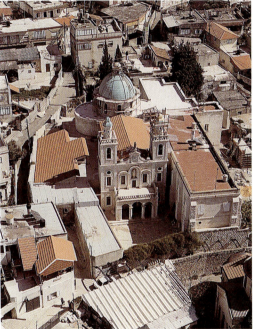

▲ Aerial view of Catholic Franciscan Church. Site of Wedding of Cana.

QUESTIONS

(1) What evidence is there to support Christian belief that Jesus performed miracles?

(2) 'Modern science says that miracles cannot happen'. How would a Christian respond to this claim?

CHAPTER TWENTY-ONE

INTERPRETING THE MIRACLES

Approach

Before studying the miracle stories, it is important to bear in mind a number of points:

- If one gets too caught up with the question of whether or not a particular event happened in exactly the way the Gospels describe it, then one can miss out on the <u>message</u> contained <u>within</u> that story. The main aim of each Gospel story, whether it concerns a miracle or not, is to help people understand who Jesus is and what he came to do.
- The Gospels contain different kinds of miracle stories. Some of these may have a greater factual content than others. Some are considered more important than others because of the insights they contain into the meaning of Jesus' life.

Why did Jesus work miracles?

The Gospel accounts reveal that:

- Jesus was often reluctant to work a miracle (see *John* 2:1–12).
- He frequently instructed those whom he healed not to tell anyone what he had done for them (see *Matthew* 9:27–31).
- He refused to use his miraculous powers either to win over the powerful (*Luke* 23:8–9) or to gain the acceptance of those unwilling to listen to his message (*Matthew* 13:54–58).

Christian scholars believe that Jesus worked miracles for three reasons:

(1) *As a response to people's faith*
At least seven miracles explicitly mention the importance of people having faith in Jesus. He responded where people truly believed in his message and

All About Faith

he worked a miracle <u>to strengthen the faith they already had</u> (read *Matthew* 8:5–13).

Jesus offered people real hope and gave them an appreciation of who God is through what he said and did.

(2) *As signs of God's love*

It was <u>compassion</u> and <u>love</u> that moved Jesus to work miracles (see *Mark* 1:40–42 and *Luke* 7:11–15). Through his actions Jesus revealed that God cares for each and every human being, regardless of their race or religion.

(3) *As signs of God's power*

Jesus worked miracles to show people that the Kingdom of which he spoke had begun in him.

For example:

- <u>When Jesus healed the sick he showed that he had the power to conquer suffering</u>.

In *Luke* 5:12–14 Jesus not only healed a man afflicted by leprosy but actually <u>touched</u> him. Lepers were social outcasts who were ordered to keep apart from other people because of the contagious nature of their disease. Jesus did something that no one else would have dared to do. He showed that while people may have rejected this man because of his illness, God had not. Jesus' actions revealed the love of God reaching out to and embracing people who were abandoned and suffering.

- <u>When Jesus cast out demons (i.e. evil spirits) he showed that the Kingdom of God can overcome every form of evil affecting people's lives.</u>

In *Mark* 5:1–20 Jesus encountered '*Legion*', a man said to have been possessed by demons. This man lived in a cemetery, cut off from his family and neighbours who were frightened by him. Jesus cast out the demons or, as some scholars think, the mental illness that had shattered this man's life and restored him to his right mind. The man was able to live with other people again and could re-build his life. Jesus' actions brought peace and hope where before there had been only rage and despair.

- <u>When Jesus showed his power over nature he revealed that God's power can do marvellous things that are both unexpected and, in human terms, thought impossible.</u>

In *John* 6:1–14 Jesus takes the five loaves and two fishes offered by a young boy and uses them to feed five thousand people who had been listening to him preach.
[N.B.] This is the <u>only</u> miracle recorded in <u>all four</u> Gospels.

In *Luke* 8:22–25 Jesus ordered the winds to cease and the waters to be calm. To the amazement of the apostles this immediately happens. This story gave great comfort to the early Christians. In times of terrible suffering, when it seemed that great waves of Roman persecution might drown them, this story reminded them that Jesus would not desert them. They had to be brave and keep their faith in him.

- <u>When Jesus restored people to life he showed that the power of God is stronger than death and that nothing can stand in the way of God's love.</u>

The Gospels tell of three occasions where Jesus raised someone from the dead: the widow of Nain's son (*Luke* 7:11–17), Jairus' daughter (*Mark* 5:21–43) and Lazarus (*John* 11:38–44).

These stories emphasise Jesus' message that <u>God can do what human beings consider impossible</u>. God can give back what seems to have been lost forever. Jesus was given power even over death. This is why Christians believe that Jesus is *the resurrection and the life*.

The importance of the miracles

Without tangible evidence of Jesus' power over sin, suffering and death, his preaching about the Kingdom of God would have been less credible to his Jewish audience.

Take for example the story of the healing of the paralysed man (see *Mark* 2:1–12 or *Luke* 5:17–26).

The pool of Bethesda in Jerusalem.

All About Faith

- The Pharisees attacked Jesus for claiming to have the power to forgive sins. They accused Jesus of *blasphemy*, i.e. showing grave disrespect by claiming to be as important as God.
- Most Jews at that time regarded physical suffering as a punishment from God for sins committed.
- They would only believe that the man's sins had been forgiven if his paralysis was removed.
- Jesus cured the man and so showed that his authority to forgive sins and his power to heal came from God.

QUESTIONS

(1) What was the main aim of each Gospel story particularly those concerning the miracles of Jesus?

(2) In what circumstances did Jesus refuse to work a miracle?

(3) Briefly state each of the three reasons why Jesus worked a miracle.

(4) What kinds of power did Jesus reveal in the four different kinds of miracle story? What does each power mean?

(5) Choose your favourite miracle story. Write a brief account of it in your own words. Explain the reasons for your choice.

(6) Why are the miracles important?

CHAPTER TWENTY-TWO

TEACHING BY PARABLES

Methods of teaching

Teaching was a vital part of Jesus' work as he travelled round the towns and villages of Palestine. He himself described it as *making God known*.

Like other rabbis of that time, Jesus used a number of different methods of teaching to get his message across:

- Question-and-answer *Matthew* 9:5; *Matthew* 16:26
- Contradictory-seeming statement *Matthew* 5:3–12; *Matthew* 10:39
- Object lesson *Matthew* 18:1–6; *Luke* 21:1–4
- Logical argument *Matthew* 22:15–45

However, Jesus is best known for his use of the parable to teach about the Kingdom of God.

What is a parable?

A parable can be defined as:
an image or story in which Jesus illustrates some point of his message by using concrete examples drawn from everyday life.

▲ Jesus teaching in the synagogue.

Importance of the parables

Much of Jesus' preaching about the Kingdom of God was done through parables. They make up about <u>a third</u> of the total content of the Gospels. It is necessary, therefore, to study them carefully if we are to gain a better understanding of Jesus' message.

All About Faith

Jesus teaching in the marketplace.

Studying the parables

The parables can be divided up into four main themes, where each group of parables is concerned with explaining an important aspect of the Kingdom of God.

[1] <u>Descriptions of God — King of the Kingdom</u>
For example, the parables of . . .

- The lost sheep *Matthew* 18:12–14
- The lost coin and the prodigal son *Luke* 15:8–32
- The labourers in the vineyard *Matthew* 20:1–16.

[2] <u>Guidance on how people should act if they hope to enter the Kingdom.</u>
For example, the parables of . . .

- The Pharisee and tax collector *Luke* 18:9–14
- The rich fool *Luke* 12:16–21
- The talents *Matthew* 25:14–30.

[3] <u>Teachings about how people should treat one another in the Kingdom.</u>
For example, the parables of . . .

- The unforgiving servant *Matthew* 18:21–35
- The good Samaritan *Luke* 10:25–37.

[4] <u>Warnings about the future day of judgement when God's Kingdom will come in all its fullness.</u>

For example, the parables of . . .

- The weeds among the wheat *Matthew* 13:24–30
- The ten bridesmaids *Matthew* 25:1–13.

Problems:

- People today are often too familiar with the parables to realise how Jesus used them to make people sit up and take notice.
- People today can have problems appreciating the depth and wisdom of the parables. Most people nowadays live in urban areas and fewer and fewer earn their living from farming. People today are not always familiar with some of the comparisons Jesus makes.

For instance, Jesus uses examples drawn from everyday life in first century Palestine:
the sower, the wineskin, the mustard tree, the fig tree and so on.
[N.B.] In order to appreciate and understand the parables we must draw upon the knowledge that archaeologists and historians have gained of the time and place in which they were originally composed.

QUESTIONS

(1) Name the <u>five</u> methods of teaching used by Jesus in the Gospels.

(2) What is a *parable*?

(3) Why is it important to study the parables?

(4) What are the problems facing a modern reader of the parables?

(5) How can the work of archaeologists and historians help us to understand their meaning?

CHAPTER TWENTY-THREE

INTERPRETING THE PARABLES

Approach

A parable is an image or story of a special kind. Indeed, a parable has often been referred to as *an earthly story with a heavenly meaning*.

This is because a parable works on two levels:

- On the surface — a parable is an interesting, easily remembered story which uses images and ideas drawn from everyday life and has a strong human interest.
- Below the surface — a parable has a deeper meaning hidden within it which Jesus wants his listeners to work out, think about and apply to their own lives.

Example 1: 'The Good Samaritan' *Luke* 10:25–37

This is the story of how a Samaritan traveller cares for a Jewish man who had been viciously attacked, robbed and left for dead. This apparently simple, straightforward tale was told to communicate some important truths about the Kingdom of God:

- Most Jews and Samaritans despised each other. Jesus wanted to challenge the attitudes of his listeners, both then and now.

— Jesus makes it clear that there is no place for racial or religious hatred in God's Kingdom. The <u>neighbour</u> whom God requires each person to love is <u>anyone in need</u>.

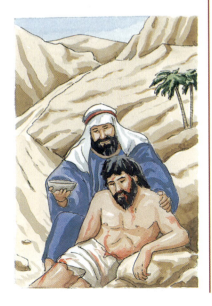

The Good Samaritan.

- Most of Jesus' listeners were quite sure that only the Jews would enter the Kingdom of God.

  — Jesus startled them by teaching that the Kingdom of God is open to everyone, whether Jewish, Samaritan or gentile.

Example 2: 'The Sower' *Luke* 8:4–15.

Here Jesus uses the simple image of a farm labourer sowing seeds to encourage his listeners to reflect on the different ways in which people respond to his message:

- The seed is the word of God.
- Those who <u>hear</u> God's word preached to them, who <u>understand</u> it and who then <u>act</u> upon it are compared to <u>good soil</u> where the seed can take root and grow.
- The seeds that fall on the pathway represent the Gospel being preached to those whose hearts and minds are closed.
- The stony ground stands for those who initially receive Jesus' message gladly, but find it makes such big demands on how they behave that they give up trying and reject it.
- The thorns represent all the worldly cares about wealth and power that can smother people's initial interest in and enthusiasm for Jesus' message.

QUESTIONS

(1) Why is a parable referred to as *an earthly story with a heavenly meaning*?

(2) In what ways did the parable of the Good Samaritan challenge the accepted ideas of most Jewish people in the time of Jesus?

(3) What message do you think the parable of the Good Samaritan contains for people today? Explain your answer.

(4) The <u>good soil</u> refers to whom in the parable of the Sower?

Example 3: 'The Prodigal Son' *Luke* 15:11–32

This is one of the best-known and most familiar of the parables. *Luke* tells us that Jesus told this story after the Pharisees had complained to him that he was spending too much time in the company of <u>sinners</u>, i.e. people who had cut themselves off from God.

The parable tells of a wealthy man with two sons, one of whom asked for his share of the family estate and then squandered it all on a wild lifestyle.

After a time the son became completely penniless and worked at the most wretched jobs to earn a living. Eventually he became truly sorry for being so <u>prodigal</u>, i.e. wasteful of all he had been given. He swallowed his pride and returned home to ask his father's forgiveness. To his astonishment, his father was delighted to have him home and forgave him. The elder brother, however, was annoyed with his father and resented his younger brother being forgiven.

- Jesus makes it quite clear that the elder brother represents the Pharisees, while the younger son represents the sinners of the world.

- The whole point of the story is that God cares deeply about all his children — both saints and sinners. God is always willing to forgive someone who is <u>genuinely</u> sorry. There are no limits to God's love.

▲ The Prodigal Son is forgiven.

Example 4:   Short sayings

There are about fifty parables in the Gospels. Some of these are only one sentence long.

Parable	Meaning
■ New cloth is not used for patching old clothes. (*Luke* 5:36)	Jesus' teaching is not simply a repeat of the old Jewish law.
■ New wine will spoil old wineskins. (*Luke* 5:37)	The teaching of Jesus will upset the traditional religious ideas and customs of the Jewish people.
■ A measure or scale used for serving others may be used also for you. (*Luke* 6:38)	A person is judged by God according to the standards that person uses to judge other people.
■ A lamp should give light. (*Luke* 8:16–18)	The Gospel message should be made known by the way Jesus' followers live their lives.

Comment: Christians believe that a modern student of Jesus' parables will find that the truths and lessons they contain are just as relevant to people's lives today as they were two thousand years ago.

Interpreting the Parables

QUESTIONS

(1) Read *Luke* 15:1–2. What complaint did the Pharisees make about Jesus?

(2) Who are the elder brother and the younger son in the parable of the prodigal son meant to represent?

(3) What is the most important point of the parable of the prodigal son?

(4) Why do Christians believe that the study of the parables is still of great importance for people today?

If we draw together all the clues about the Kingdom of God found in the Gospels, we can construct the following diagram showing its many aspects:

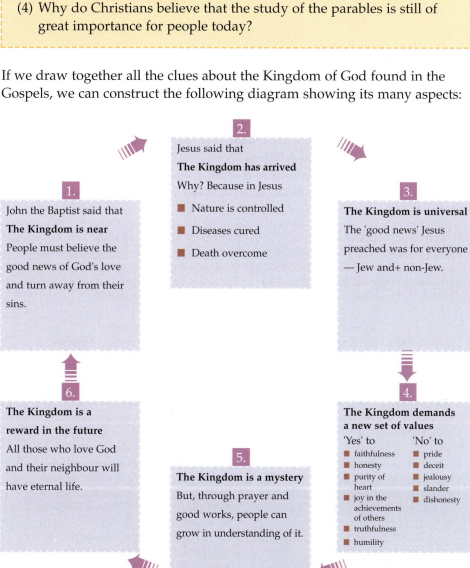

CHAPTER TWENTY-FOUR

JESUS' ENTRY INTO JERUSALEM

Holy Week

The events of the last week of Jesus' ministry, known as Holy Week are treated in far greater detail than any other part of his life. The evangelists did this to emphasise the central importance of Jesus' suffering, death and resurrection for the Christian religion.

The following outline of events in that final incident-packed week of Jesus' life, as been drawn from the information offered by the four evangelists:

Sunday	Wednesday
Jesus arrived in Jerusalem seated on a colt and was welcomed by cheering crowds waving palm branches and shouting 'Hosanna'.	Judas Iscariot, one of Jesus' apostles went to the Jewish authorities with an offer to betray Jesus so that he could be quietly arrested.
Monday	**Thursday**
Jesus went to the Temple and denounced the traders and money-changers. Jesus overturned their stalls and drove them out of the Temple. The Pharisees and the Sadducees in the Sanhedrin plotted to kill Jesus.	Jesus shared an evening meal with his disciples. Judas left early. Later, in the Garden of Gethsemane, Judas arrived with the Temple police who arrested Jesus. Judas identified him for them.
Tuesday	**Friday**
Jesus taught in the Temple and was asked some leading questions intended to trap him: ■ by the Pharisees (about his authority and about his views on Roman taxation) ■ by the Sadducees (about his views on the possibility of life after death, which they did not believe in).	During the early hours Jesus was interrogated by the Sanhedrin and later put on trial by the Roman governor, Pontius Pilate. Jesus was scourged and condemned to death by crucifixion. Jesus was nailed to an upright cross and suffered an agonising death. His body was buried in a tomb nearby.

Why did Jesus go to Jerusalem?

For several years Jesus healed and taught people. Then probably in the spring of 30 A.D., his ministry reached its climax. Jesus had come to a great moment of decision. Either:

- He could return home to the safety of Galilee,

or

- He could go on to Jerusalem where his life would be in danger because the things he had said and done had earned him powerful enemies.

Jesus decided that he had to go to Jerusalem. It was the capital city and site of the Temple — Judaism's most holy place. The Sanhedrin was there. Jerusalem was the centre of political and religious power in Palestine. Jesus was determined to teach and heal there.

Jesus arrived in Jerusalem as preparations were beginning for the annual feast of *Passover*, when the Jews celebrated God's freeing of their ancestors from slavery in Egypt. Most Jews believed that Passover was the time when the long-awaited Messiah would reveal himself. Everything Jesus had said and done led up to this moment.

▲ Jerusalem, road leading down from the Mount of Olives, and the Dome of the Rock across the Kidron Valley.

Revealing himself

Until this point Jesus had repeatedly told his disciples <u>not</u> to publicly state that he was the Messiah, (see *Luke* 9:21, *Mark* 8:30 and *Matthew* 16:20). Finally, Jesus decided that the time had arrived to go to Jerusalem and reveal that he was the Messiah.

While journeying to Jerusalem, Jesus had several discussions with his disciples about his actions and mission. It seems that they still did not understand the true nature of Jesus' messiahship (see *Mark* 10:35–45 and *Matthew* 20:20–28). They still seem to have expected him to become a powerful political ruler of a new independent Jewish kingdom. However, Jesus made it quite clear that he came into the world <u>to serve others</u> and not to be served. Anyone who wanted to be his disciple would have to be <u>humble</u> and <u>willing to endure great suffering</u>.

It was only after Jesus had risen from the dead that the apostles began to understand the meaning of what Jesus had said to them.

Jerusalem in the time of Jesus.
▼

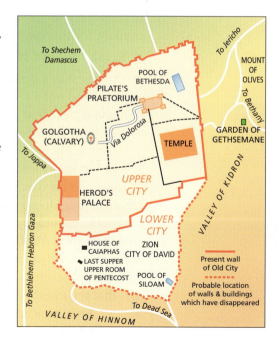

All About Faith

QUESTIONS

(1) What is the name given to the last week in the life of Jesus?
(2) What is the feast of *Passover*?
(3) What did many Jews believe about the Passover and the coming of the Messiah?
(4) After repeatedly telling his disciples not to publicly call him the Messiah, why did Jesus finally decide to go to Jerusalem for the feast of Passover?
(5) Did his disciples understand the true meaning of what Jesus had said and done <u>before</u> or <u>after</u> his death and resurrection?

Palm Sunday

See: *John* 12:12–19, *Luke* 19:28–40, *Mark* 11:1–11, *Matthew* 21:1–11.

The Gospel accounts tell us that Jesus joined the procession of pilgrims entering Jerusalem for the festival.

Aware, however, that most Jews were expecting the Messiah to be a <u>warrior king</u> like King David in the *Old Testament*, Jesus made it clear that he had no political ambitions. He did not arrive in glittering style trying to impress people. Instead, he entered Jerusalem seated on a colt or young donkey, for two reasons:

- To fulfil the *Old Testament* prophecy in *Zachariah* 9:9–10 about the Messiah.
- The colt was a humble animal of peace and not a war-horse. This made it clear that Jesus would rule over people by peace and not by violence. He invited people to follow him but never forced them.

Jesus and his disciples entered the city from the Mount of Olives and he was enthusiastically greeted by a large crowd. In *John*, *Mark* and *Matthew*'s accounts, many pilgrims greeted Jesus with palm branches. It is because of this that the event is known as *Palm Sunday*. Jesus was acclaimed 'King of Israel' and the people shouted out

Jesus entering Jerusalem, on a donkey. People lay branches of palm trees in his wake. ➡

'hosanna' meaning *'save now'* (see *John* 12:13). This welcome was like the coronation procession for a new king.

QUESTIONS

(1) Why did Jesus enter Jerusalem seated on a colt?
(2) Why is the first day of Holy Week known as *'Palm Sunday'*?
(3) What does *hosanna* mean?

Reactions

While Jesus was enthusiastically greeted by large crowds of pilgrims, others observing this scene were far from happy. Influential members of the Sanhedrin were worried that Jesus would upset the delicate political peace in Jerusalem. The city was crowded with easily excited pilgrims who were very anti-Roman and who longed for the promised Messiah to appear. There was great tension in the air and it was feared that the Zealots would be only too ready to take advantage of any opportunity to begin a revolt.

The Romans, however, do not appear to have considered Jesus a threat at this stage. Their spies would probably have informed them that Jesus had no political ambitions. They may have just viewed him as a strange religious figure who, if he did become a problem, would best be dealt with by the Jewish authorities.

Conflict

Before he set out for Jerusalem, Jesus shocked his disciples by predicting that he would be put to death (*Luke* 18:31–34, *Mark* 10:32–34, *Matthew* 20:17–19 and *John* 12:23–33). During the three years of his ministry, Jesus had won over many devoted followers. However, he had also made some devoted <u>enemies</u>, most notably among the Pharisees.

The evangelists record a number of occasions on which Jesus clashed with the Pharisees:

- The healing of the paralysed man (*Luke* 5:17–25).
- The casting out of an evil spirit (*Mark* 3:20–30).
- The call of Matthew or Levi (*Matthew* 9:9–13).
- The incident in the cornfield (*Luke* 6:1–5).
- The healing of the man with a withered hand (*Luke* 6:6–11).
- The healing of the man born blind (*John* 9:13–41).

The Pharisees considered themselves to be <u>the</u> greatest experts on God's law. Jesus shocked them by claiming for himself a position of authority <u>above them</u>. While a few Pharisees such as Nicodemus and Joseph of Arimathea supported Jesus, most opposed him. When Jesus revealed his authority by healing and restoring people to life, they reacted with a combination of fear and anger.

The Pharisees made four accusations against Jesus:
- That he committed <u>blasphemy</u> when he forgave people's sins, because only God could do such a thing.
- That Jesus received his powers from the devil.
- That he broke the Sabbath laws prohibiting work by healing the sick.
- That Jesus was unfit to be called 'rabbi' because he mixed with 'unclean' people such as non-Jews and social outcasts. The Pharisees believed that proper Jews should keep themselves separate as God's chosen people.

Jesus responded to these charges by declaring:
- That, as the <u>Son of Man</u>, he had the authority to forgive sins.
- That his power to restore life and health <u>came from God</u>.
- That he was <u>the Lord of the Sabbath</u>.
- That his mission was to <u>reveal God's love</u> to outcasts and declared that <u>all</u> people were invited to enter the Kingdom of God — saints and sinners, Jews and non-Jews.

These responses by Jesus infuriated his enemies. But Jesus went even further. He called these Pharisees <u>hypocrites</u> who had replaced love of God with a cold-hearted obsession with petty rule-keeping. They had closed their hearts to God's message. A showdown between Jesus and his enemies was inevitable.

QUESTIONS

(1) Why were influential members of the Sanhedrin worried by Jesus' entry into Jerusalem?

(2) Was Jesus aware that his life was in danger?

(3) Did any Pharisees support Jesus?

(4) Imagine you are an influential Pharisee in the Sanhedrin. Write out your reasons for opposing Jesus.

Jesus' Entry into Jerusalem

The Temple: Judaism's most holy place

History of the Temple

There were two great temples in the history of Judaism. The first temple was built by Solomon (961–922 B.C.). This, however, was lost in the destruction of Jerusalem in 587 B.C. A second temple was built around 515 B.C. Under Herod the Great (37–4 B.C.) this Temple was enlarged. Work had begun in 20 B.C. and ten years later the Temple was dedicated. However, it was only finally completed by A.D. 64.

Herod's Temple.

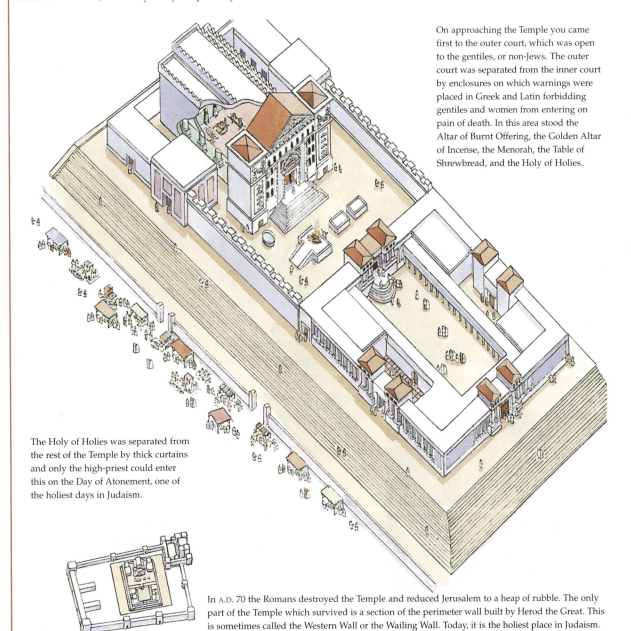

On approaching the Temple you came first to the outer court, which was open to the gentiles, or non-Jews. The outer court was separated from the inner court by enclosures on which warnings were placed in Greek and Latin forbidding gentiles and women from entering on pain of death. In this area stood the Altar of Burnt Offering, the Golden Altar of Incense, the Menorah, the Table of Shrewbread, and the Holy of Holies.

The Holy of Holies was separated from the rest of the Temple by thick curtains and only the high-priest could enter this on the Day of Atonement, one of the holiest days in Judaism.

In A.D. 70 the Romans destroyed the Temple and reduced Jerusalem to a heap of rubble. The only part of the Temple which survived is a section of the perimeter wall built by Herod the Great. This is sometimes called the Western Wall or the Wailing Wall. Today, it is the holiest place in Judaism.

Source: 'Sunday Message' 15.11.1998.

CHAPTER TWENTY-FIVE

JESUS IN THE TEMPLE

Israel. Orthodox Jews praying at the Western Wall. ➡

Jesus cleanses the Temple

According to the earliest Gospel account, *Mark* 11:15–18, Jesus went to the Temple on the Monday of Holy Week (see also *Luke* 19:45–48 *Matthew* 21:12–13 and *John* 2:12–22). What he found there both appalled and deeply angered him. To understand why Jesus reacted in this way, we need to know how the Jews worshipped God in the Temple.

All pilgrims to the Temple were expected to give the Temple priests an animal which would then be killed and burned as a sacrifice (i.e. offering) to God. For example, in *Luke* 2:24 Mary and Joseph gave a pair of doves as a sacrifice when they presented Jesus for circumcision.

Denarius with the head of Tiberius (42-37 A.D.). ▼

However, only animals *without any imperfections* (see *Leviticus* 1:3) were acceptable as sacrifices. Such animals could be bought in the market that the Temple authorities had allowed to be set up in the Court of Gentiles, but at a higher price than elsewhere.

However, Jews could not purchase any of these acceptable animals with their everyday money. All silver coins in circulation bore the image of the Roman emperor. Jews were forbidden to make an image of anyone (see *Exodus* 20:4), especially someone who claimed to be a god. These coins could not be used to buy an animal acceptable for sacrifice.

Instead Jewish pilgrims had to go to the stalls of

money-changers who had also been permitted into the Court of Gentiles. These money-changers exchanged the people's everyday coins for special Temple coins with which they could buy an animal for sacrifice. These money-changers charged a high price for exchanging pilgrims' coins.

Seeing how devout pilgrims were being exploited by such unscrupulous people, Jesus decided to drive them out of the Temple area. It was supposed to be *a house of prayer* and *a light to the gentiles*. They had turned it into a den of profiteering. Jesus over-turned their tables and drove out their animals.

This whole scene was undoubtedly observed by the Temple priests who were among the most influential members of the Sadducees. Jesus had openly attacked the corrupt practices that they had allowed to thrive within the Temple's precincts. Jesus had publicly embarrassed them and had shown them to have failed to uphold the high standards they demanded of everyone else.

The Sadducees agreed with the Pharisees. They could not tolerate anyone who showed them up and challenged their authority in such a manner.

The cleansing of the Temple seemed to have finally convinced the leading Sadducees and Pharisees in the Sanhedrin to find some way to have Jesus put to death.

▲ El Greco's Expulsion of traders from Temple (traders on left, apostles on right).

QUESTIONS

(1) What was the role played by animals in Jewish Temple worship in the time of Jesus?

(2) Where in the Temple did the Jewish authorities allow a market to be set up?

(3) Why did Jews have to exchange their everyday silver coins to buy an animal for sacrifice?

(4) What were the animal traders and money-changers doing that so angered Jesus?

(5) Why were the Jewish authorities angered by Jesus' cleansing of the Temple?

Attempts to trap Jesus

Over the next few days Jesus taught and healed people in the Temple. He attracted large crowds. The leading members of the Sanhedrin could not ignore Jesus' growing popularity. However, they could not openly act against him without causing a riot. So they tried to trap him by getting him to say something that they could use to have him arrested.

The evangelists record two instances of this:
- The question of the Pharisees about paying taxes to Caesar (see *Luke* 20:20–26).
- The question of the Sadducees about marriage and life after death (see *Luke* 20:27–40).

In each case, Jesus out-witted his opponents and made important statements about both subjects.

- In the first instance Jesus knew that the Pharisees were hoping that he would say that it was against the Law of Moses to pay taxes to the Roman emperor. If he did then he could be arrested on a charge of *sedition*, i.e. encouraging opposition to Roman rule.

  The answer which Jesus gave left them with no excuse to condemn him as a political trouble-maker:

  'pay Caesar what belongs to Caesar and pay God what belongs to God'
  (*Mark* 12:17).

  Jesus made it clear that a person can be faithful in his/her duties both to God and to the state. They need not cancel each other out.

- In the second instance Jesus responded to a question raised by the Sadducees, who did not believe in life after death. Jesus rebuked them for their shallow line of reasoning and limited vision. He told them that marriage is for this life only and that the next life is very different in nature: there those who have followed God's way will live in a community of perfect love where the differences that separate people in this life will no longer matter.

The parable of the Tenants in the Vineyard

(see *Mark* 12:1–12 and *Luke* 20:9–19)

Jesus told this story to the pilgrims gathered in the Temple. The image of the Jewish people as the vineyard of God dates back to *Isaiah* 5:1–7 and was very familiar to Jesus' listeners. This parable is *an allegory*, i.e. a story in which the events and characters all have another meaning.

- The vineyard (Israel) is good and it belongs to the landlord (God).
- The tenants (Jewish leaders) are responsible for looking after the vineyard.
- These tenants ill-treat the servants (Old Testament prophets) sent by the landlord to collect his share of the harvest.
- The tenants reject and kill the landlord's son (Jesus).
- The landlord is likely to hand the vineyard over to others (gentiles) who are more deserving.

The Pharisees and Sadducees knew exactly what Jesus meant. He was clearly implying that they had neglected their responsibilities towards the people. This made them even more determined to arrest Jesus.

QUESTIONS

(1) State the two occasions in the Temple where (a) the Pharisees and (b) the Sadducees tried to undermine Jesus' teaching before the Jewish people.
(2) Read *Luke* 20:20–26. What point do you think Jesus was making?
(3) What is an *allegory*?
(4) Why did the parable of the Tenants in the Vineyard so anger the Pharisees and the Sadducees?

Betrayal

The Sadducees and the Pharisees wanted to arrest Jesus. Although he had not broken any laws, they were determined to find some way to have him put to death. However, they could not make any attempt to arrest Jesus during daylight for fear of triggering a riot. So they decided to arrest him after dark, someplace out of public view (see *Matthew* 26:3–5). To do this they would need inside help. This was provided by one of the apostles — Judas Iscariot.

Judas had witnessed all the good Jesus had done. He had been one of Jesus' close circle of friends. Yet, in spite of all this, he betrayed Jesus. Why?

Explanations

Generally scholars have tended to support one or other of the following explanations for this act of betrayal.

[1] [Judas was a greedy and disloyal opportunist who sold out his friend to make money and gain influential contacts in the Sanhedrin.]

The Synoptic Gospel accounts all agree that Judas approached the Sanhedrin's key figures and <u>volunteered his help</u>:

> 'Judas went to the chief priests and officers of the Temple guard and discussed with them how he might betray Jesus. They were delighted and agreed to give him money. He agreed and watched for an opportunity to hand Jesus over to them when no crowd was present.'
> Luke 22:4–6.

[2] [Judas was not treacherous but <u>misguided</u>]

Why did Judas commit suicide after hearing that Jesus had been condemned to death? One evangelist offers the following account:

> 'When he found out that Jesus had been condemned, Judas his betrayer was filled with remorse and took the thirty pieces of silver back to the chief priests and elders. "I have sinned", he said, "I have betrayed innocent blood". "What is that to us?", they replied, "that is your responsibility". And flinging down the silver pieces in the Temple, he went away and hanged himself.'
> Matthew 27:3–5.

Obviously Judas was horrified to realise what he had done. But what exactly had he intended to do in the first place?

Thirty silver coins was the price of a slave. Surely a small sum to receive for handing over someone whom the Sanhedrin considered to be such a serious threat. Why did Judas accept such a modest payment? Was the money ever really an issue?

Some scholars believe that a clue might be found in Judas' surname which may have meant <u>man of the Sicarii</u>, a small violent Zealot group. Did Judas wrongly believe that the 'Kingdom of God' which Jesus had preached would be an independent Jewish kingdom ruled over by Jesus himself? Did Judas conclude that all he had to do was force Jesus to go before the Sanhedrin and that then Jesus would convince them that he was the Messiah? Did he think that Jesus would work a miracle if he knew his life was in danger? Could Judas really have been so blind to the truth? Perhaps. Perhaps not. We cannot say for certain.

Judas receives the thirty pieces of silver. Painting on the ceiling of the Church at Zillis, Switzerland.
▼

QUESTIONS

(1) Why did the Jewish authorities want help from someone inside Jesus' circle of followers?

(2) Explain briefly the two theories about why Judas betrayed Jesus.

(3) Which of these two explanations do you find the most convincing? Give reasons for your answer.

CHAPTER TWENTY-SIX

THE LAST SUPPER

Staying on course

Jesus realised that his life was in grave danger. This is quite clear in the accounts of his being anointed by a woman at Bethany, a village near Jerusalem (see *Mark* 14:3–9 and *Matthew* 26:6–13). It would have been an understandable reaction if Jesus had left Jerusalem then and avoided further conflict. But he chose to stay. Jesus did not do this because he knew that he would rise from the dead but because he wanted to stay true to all that he had believed and taught.

The Last Supper

On the evening before he was put to death, Jesus shared a private meal with his closest friends. It was held in a room loaned to them by a follower in Jerusalem. This event has since become known as *the Last Supper*.

Although the Synoptic Gospels describe it as a seder (i.e. Passover meal), many modern scholars accept instead the dating of *John* 13:1. The Last Supper took place on the Thursday evening before the great feast of Passover (which would begin at 6 p.m. on Friday evening).

At the end of the meal and according to the normal Jewish custom, Jesus said a prayer of thanksgiving to God for the meal they had shared. Then he did something unexpected.

He took the bread, blessed and broke it, gave some to his friends and said:

> 'This is my body given for you; do this in remembrance of me.'
> Luke 22:19.

Then, after they had eaten this, he took a cup of wine and after blessing it, gave it to them and said:

> 'Drink from it, all of you. This is my blood, the blood of the new covenant, which is poured out for many for the forgiveness of sins.'
> Matthew 26:28

By these words and actions, Jesus forewarned his friends of his approaching death and clearly connected this meal with his death.

The disciples' reaction

The disciples present that evening were puzzled. Jesus had used the language of *sacrifice,* i.e. offering something of value up to God. Jesus had said that the breaking of the bread and the pouring out of the wine symbolised (i.e. stood for) his impending death. He had told them that he was going to give his life for them. The disciples were confused and upset by this.

The disciples were quite aware of the increasing risk to Jesus' life but all the confrontations of the previous days seem to have made them more confident that Jesus had come to Jerusalem to assume his role as king. They had not expected him to be killed.

It was only after Jesus' death and resurrection that they came to understand the meaning of what Jesus had said and done that Thursday evening. He was telling them that his death would be no ordinary death. Through his death, God would do something great.

QUESTIONS

(1) (a) On what day of Holy Week did the Last Supper take place?
    (b) How is this known?
(2) Read *Luke* 22:19 and *Matthew* 26:28. By using such words and actions what message was Jesus giving his disciples?
(3) Why were the disciples puzzled by what Jesus had said and done?

The meaning of the Last Supper

The Last Supper was held on the evening before the feast of Passover. The disciples, as Jews, later made the link between the Last Supper and that Jewish feast.

At the time of the Exodus, the Hebrews were told to sacrifice a lamb and mark the door of their homes with its blood. As a result they were spared in the terrible events that followed. The blood of the lamb was the sign of God's covenant with the Hebrews to set them free and restore their homeland to them.

The *Old Testament* prophet Jeremiah (see *Jeremiah* 31:31–34) had taught that one day God would replace this agreement he had made with Moses with a new covenant. At the Last Supper, Jesus said that his day had finally arrived. His blood — his life — would be poured out on the cross as the sign of God's new covenant. By giving his life Jesus would reveal the extraordinary depth of God's love. Through his death, the broken relationship between God and human beings would be restored and healed. Through his death, God and humankind would be brought back together and become <u>at one</u>. This idea is called '<u>atonement</u>'.

The Mass

For nearly two thousand years since Holy Thursday, Christians all over the world have followed Jesus' command to *'do this in remembrance of me'*. They have gathered together to solemnly repeat Jesus' words and gestures and recall the events of his life, death and resurrection. They celebrate what Catholics call the Mass or what Protestants call the Holy Communion service. This is a topic to which we shall return later and examine in greater detail.

Priest celebrating mass today.

The fourth Gospel

Jesus washing the feet of the disciples.

The Gospel of *John* does not mention the details of the Last Supper itself. The fourth evangelist recalls the story of how Jesus washed the feet of his disciples.

John 13:1–17 reminds Christians that they can only truly call themselves Christians when they are willing to put others first. They must be willing to live by God's standards.

> 'I give you a new commandment, that you love one another. Just as I have loved you, you also should love one another.'
> John 13:34.

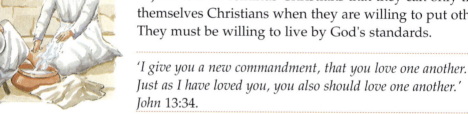

QUESTIONS

(1) What was the shedding of the lamb's blood at the Jewish feast of Passover meant to represent?

(2) What had the prophet Jeremiah taught about God's covenant?

(3) What was the meaning of Jesus shedding his blood on the cross?

(4) What is the meaning of <u>atonement</u>?

CHAPTER TWENTY-SEVEN

THE ARREST AND INTERROGATION

Betrayed

After the Last Supper, Jesus and his disciples went outside the city to the Garden of Gethsemane, near the Mount of Olives. Jesus went there to pray for the strength to endure the terrible suffering he knew lay ahead (see *Luke* 22:39–46).

It was at this point that Judas arrived with a group of men *'armed with swords and cudgels'* (*Matthew* 26:47) to arrest Jesus. According to *John* 18:3 this was a contingent of Temple guards led by some of the Temple priests.

Jesus challenged their right to do this. He pointed out how he had taught in public each day in the Temple but that none of them had the courage to arrest him there. Instead, they came to arrest him under cover of darkness when no one could see what they were doing (see *Luke* 22:53).

Jesus and the disciples could have resisted arrest and might have been able to escape into the night. But Jesus undoubtedly realised that his enemies would never cease to pursue him because he posed such a threat to them. They would simply capture him another day. To save lives, Jesus stopped his disciples from fighting to prevent his arrest (see *Matthew* 26:51).

When Peter drew his sword and cut off the ear of the high priest's servant (see *John* 18:10), Jesus immediately stepped in to halt the violence and healed the wounded man (see *Luke* 22:49–51). Although his own life was in great danger, Jesus still tried to bring peace and healing, even to those who considered him to be their mortal enemy.

Judas arriving with a group of men 'armed with swords and cudgels' to arrest Jesus.

All About Faith

Peter's denial

When Jesus was arrested, most of the disciples fled (see *Mark* 14:50). Peter, however, followed the arrest detail to find out what was going to happen to Jesus.

Jesus had startled Peter at the Last Supper by predicting that soon <u>Peter would publicly deny having ever known him</u>. Peter was so upset at Jesus saying this that he promised to face death alongside Jesus (see *Mark* 14:29–31). When the test came, however, Peter failed. He gravely underestimated the sheer heart-clenching terror he would experience when faced with the threat of interrogation and execution. Jesus, in contrast, was quite aware of all this.

While Jesus was being interrogated by the Sanhedrin, Peter remained in the courtyard outside. When identified as a follower of Jesus on three occasions, Peter vehemently denied it. *Luke* records something the other accounts do not mention: After Peter had denied Jesus, he turned around to see Jesus looking straight at him. At that moment a cock crowed and Peter was crushed by the realisation that what Jesus had said had come to pass. Peter had denied ever knowing his best friend. Peter went away and wept bitterly (see *Luke* 22:54–62).

Peter denies knowing Jesus.

QUESTIONS

(1) Where was Jesus arrested?

(2) Who led the group of Temple guards which arrested Jesus?

(3) Why did Jesus allow himself to be arrested?

(4) Read *Luke* 22:49–51. What point is the evangelist making about Jesus?

(5) What did Jesus predict about Peter at the Last Supper? How did Peter react when Jesus said this?

(6) Imagine that you are Peter the Apostle. Write an account of your role in the events of Holy Thursday evening and Good Friday morning.

Sequence of events

After his arrest Jesus went through a series of interrogations before he was finally tried and condemned to death.

(1) Interrogation by Annas, the former high priest *John* 18:12–14 and 19–24.

(2) Interrogation by Caiaphas, the current high priest *Matthew* 26:57, *Mark* 14:53 and *John* 18:24.

(3) Court of Inquiry before the Sanhedrin *Matthew* 26:59–66, *Mark* 14:55–64 and *Luke* 22:66–71.

(4) Trial before Pontius Pilate, the Roman Governor, Part One: *Matthew* 27:1–2 and 11–14, *Mark* 15:2–5, *Luke* 23:1–4 and *John* 18:28–38.

(5) Interrogation by Herod Antipas, ruler of Galilee *Luke* 23:6–12.

(6) Trial before Pontius Pilate, the Roman Governor, Part Two: *Matthew* 27:15–26, *Mark* 15:6–15, *Luke* 23:13–25 and *John* 18:39–19:16.

The court of inquiry

After some preliminary questioning by Annas and Caiaphas, Jesus was brought before the seventy members of the Sanhedrin. They met in 'the Hall of Hewn Stones' in the inner court of the Temple. They sat in a semi-circle and were presided over by Caiaphas, *'the high priest that year'* (*John* 18:13).

This was more a court of inquiry than a trial. Its main purpose was to decide what charge the Jewish leaders would make against Jesus in the trial that would be held later by the Roman governor.

The method adopted by the Sanhedrin showed no respect for Jesus' right to a fair hearing.

- Instead of charging Jesus with some offence and calling witnesses, they questioned Jesus in the hope that he would condemn himself by his own words.
- It was not considered legal to hold either a trial or an inquiry such as this at night.
- Jesus was beaten and abused both before his questioning (*Luke* 22:63–65) and during it (*John* 18:22).

This is perhaps not surprising. The Sanhedrin's leadership had already made up their minds. They wanted Jesus put to death. Both the Sadducees and the Pharisees had their reasons for wanting this:

- Jesus had publicly challenged the authority of the Sadducees and had exposed their low standards when he cleansed the Temple.

All About Faith

- Jesus had repeatedly challenged the authority of the Pharisees and had exposed their hypocrisy over the interpretation of the law.
- Jesus claimed to be the Messiah. Both the Sadducees and the Pharisees feared he might encourage a popular uprising against the Romans.
- Caiaphas had been high priest for twelve years. At any time he could have been fired at will by the Roman governor. He had only lasted that long by being quick to remove any threat to the peace and by keeping good relations with Rome. He considered Jesus a threat.

During his interrogation Jesus was accused of wanting to destroy the Temple. This was quite obviously not what Jesus had wanted to happen. Moreover, the witnesses brought forward to support this allegation contradicted each other. According to Jewish law, if witnesses disagreed in such a fashion, then a trial or inquiry was supposed to end. But the Sanhedrin would not let Jesus go free.

Throughout all of this Jesus listened and remained silent. He knew it was pointless to reply. They were only interested in condemning him. They wanted Jesus to declare himself to be the Messiah so that they could go to the Roman governor and have Jesus condemned as a political trouble-maker.

It seems that Caiaphas became more and more frustrated as the proceedings dragged on and Jesus refused to answer the false accusations made against him. Finally Caiaphas asked Jesus directly:

> 'Are you the Messiah, the Son of the Blessed One?'
> (Mark 14:61)

Jesus chose, at last, to respond, answering:

> 'I am. And you will see the Son of Man sitting at the right hand of the Mighty One and coming on the clouds of heaven.'
> (Mark 14:62)

In giving this answer, Jesus not only identified himself as the Messiah, but went on to say that he shared a unique relationship with God and was beyond even the authority of the Sanhedrin.

The Sanhedrin members were infuriated by this and decided that Jesus had committed *blasphemy*, i.e. he had claimed for himself a dignity due to God alone. It was not Jesus' claim to be the Messiah that really angered them but his claim to be in some way divine (see *Mark* 14:63–65, *Matthew* 26:64–66 and *Luke* 22:67–70). Although the Sanhedrin wanted to put Jesus to death, they no longer had the legal power to impose the death penalty on him. This power was in the hands of the Roman governor (see *John* 18:31).

QUESTIONS

(1) Read *John* 18:13. Who was the High Priest?

(2) What was the main purpose of the court of inquiry held by the Sanhedrin?

(3) Do you think that Jesus was given a fair hearing by the Sanhedrin? Give reasons for your answer.

(4) Why did many of the Sanhedrin members want Jesus put to death?

(5) What should have happened when the witnesses called against Jesus contradicted each other?

(6) Why do you think Jesus remained silent throughout his interrogation?

(7) What is *blasphemy*?

(8) Read *Mark* 14:61–62. Why did Jesus' reply so anger the Sanhedrin?

(9) Why did the Sanhedrin hand Jesus over for trial by the Roman governor?

Model of Jerusalem at the time of Second Temple. The Temple and the Porticoes.

CHAPTER TWENTY-EIGHT

THE TRIAL OF JESUS

Introduction

Model of Pilate's residence in Jerusalem. A detail of the Antonia fortress.

Pontius Pilate, the Roman governor, was staying at the Antonia fortress near the Temple complex. Shortly after dawn on what Christians call *Good Friday* morning, a delegation from the Sanhedrin brought Jesus before Pilate. Although the Sanhedrin had declared Jesus guilty of blasphemy, this was a religious matter which would be of no interest to Pilate. If the Jewish leaders wanted the Romans to execute Jesus for them, then they would have to convince Pilate that Jesus posed a danger to Roman rule over Palestine.

The charges against Jesus

The delegation from the Sanhedrin accused Jesus of <u>treason</u> which was the most serious political offence. They claimed that:

- Jesus had proclaimed himself <u>Messiah</u> and called himself *King of the Jews*.
- He had told the people not to pay their taxes to the emperor.
- He had disturbed the peace and might soon lead a revolt. (see *Luke* 23:2 and 5).

Pontius Pilate was not the kind of man who needed much persuading to condemn a person to death if he believed that he/she was a threat. It is estimated that there were six thousand executions during his time as governor (A.D. 26 to 36).

Pilate's response

Pilate was trained in Roman law. The Gospel accounts show that, after Pilate had examined the evidence presented by the Jewish authorities to support their accusation, he concluded that Jesus was innocent (see *Luke* 23:4 and *John* 18:38).

Yet Pilate was worried about offending the Sanhedrin. He did not want to condemn Jesus but he wanted to save face. On hearing that Jesus came from Galilee, he sent him to be questioned by Herod Antipas, the ruler of Galilee (see *Luke* 23:6–12).

Herod Antipas

Herod had heard about Jesus and tried to force him to work a miracle for him. When Jesus refused either to say or do anything, Herod let his guards dress Jesus in a purple robe and make fun of the idea that Jesus was a king. Then he sent Jesus back to Pilate.

Pilate questions Jesus

The Roman governor was still satisfied that Jesus posed no threat. But to clarify matters beyond all doubt he asked Jesus a direct question:
'Are you the king of the Jews?'

Jesus responded:
'Yes, I am a king.' John 18:37.

However, Jesus explained his words by adding:
'Mine is not a kingdom of this world; if my kingdom were of this world, my men would have fought to prevent my being surrendered to the Jews. But my kingdom is not of this kind.'
John 18:36.

▲ Jesus before Pilate, accused of treason by Chief Priests.

Pilate found Jesus' calm manner both impressive and disturbing. He was quite unsure what to do next. He realised that there was no case against Jesus and *'was anxious to set him free'* (John 19:12). But, the Sanhedrin's representatives were becoming angrier as each moment passed. In an effort to pacify them Pilate stated:
'As you can see, the man has done nothing that deserves death, so I shall have him flogged and then let him go.'
John 23:15–16.

A Roman scourging was a horrific experience: the victim was tied to a post and then repeatedly struck upon the back by a multi-stranded whip, which had

Roman whip of the kind used to scourge Jesus.

pieces of jagged metal inserted into each leather strand, so that the lashes not only cut the skin, but tore strips of flesh off each time they made contact. A severe scourging could kill a person.

Jesus or Barabbas

But, Pilate under-estimated the determination of the High Priest and the Sanhedrin. They wanted Jesus dead. It was as simple as that. Then, Pilate pulled what he thought was a master stroke. Over the years it had become the accepted practice for the Roman Governor to release a Jewish prisoner during a major religious feast. To honour the feast of Passover, Pilate offered the crowd gathered outside the Antonia Fortress a choice: he would allow them to choose the one to be released. He offered them either Jesus or a violent rebel named Barabbas. Pilate was surprised when the crowd shouted for Barabbas to be set free. One evangelist claims that the crowd had been put up or bribed to do this by the Jewish leaders (*Mark* 15:11).

Pilate was forced to set Barabbas free in order to avoid a riot (*Mark* 15:15).

Jesus is condemned to death

Pilate still hesitated, however, to condemn Jesus (see *Luke* 23:20–22). Then the Sanhedrin delegates uttered words that must have chilled Pilate to the bone:
'If you let this man go, you are no friend of Caesar. Anyone who claims to be a king is an enemy of Caesar.' *John* 19:12.

They were threatening to report Pilate to the Emperor Tiberius for failing to execute someone whom they claimed was a threat to Roman rule of Palestine. Pilate was no doubt afraid that he might be recalled to Rome and might lose his job or even his life, especially if Tiberius thought Pilate had allowed Jesus to set himself up as a rival to the emperor.

At this point Pilate caved in to the Sanhedrin's demand and declared Jesus guilty of treason.

Pilate gives Jesus to the people, beaten and bloody.

The Trial of Jesus

He knew that:
'the chief priests had handed Jesus over to him because they were jealous.'
Mark 15:10.
He knew that Jesus had not committed any crime.

In a dramatic, public gesture by which Pilate tried to distance himself from the whole event:
'He took water and washed his hands in front of the crowd. "I am innocent of this man's blood", he said. "It is your responsibility."'
Matthew 27:24.

But this gesture could not alter the fact that Pilate was first and foremost interested in saving his job. To do this he <u>knowingly condemned an innocent man to death</u>.

QUESTIONS

(1) When the Sanhedrin brought Jesus before Pontius Pilate, what political offence did they accuse Jesus of committing?

(2) Read *Luke* 23:2 and 5. What were the three things they accused Jesus of doing?

(3) Why did Pilate send Jesus to be questioned by Herod Antipas?

(4) How did Herod and his guards treat Jesus?

(5) Read *John* 18:36. If you were Pilate, how would you have understood Jesus' words? Would you have considered him a threat to Roman rule? Explain your answer.

(6) What was a <u>scourging</u>?

(7) Why do you think Pilate offered the crowd outside the Antonia fortress a choice between freeing Jesus or Barabbas?

(8) Why do you think Pilate was surprised by the reaction of the crowd?

(9) Read *John* 19:12. In what way did the Sanhedrin delegates threaten Pilate? How did Pilate react?

(10) Read *Matthew* 27:24. What did Pilate do? Why did he do this?

CHAPTER TWENTY-NINE

THE CRUCIFIXION AND DEATH OF JESUS

Introduction

See *Mark* 15:16–41 *Luke* 23:26–49 *Matthew* 27:27–56 *John* 19:16–37

The story of Jesus' crucifixion is so familiar to us that it is quite easy to forget how truly awful it was to die on a cross. It was a barbaric form of execution reserved for non-Romans found guilty of treason. Crucifixion caused the condemned person to suffer an agonising and lingering death. This was to deter other people from challenging the authority of Rome.

Carrying the cross

Carrying the cross into the Holy Sepulchre on Good Friday in Jerusalem.
▼

Contrary to the way in which artists over the centuries have depicted the crucifixion, historians believe that Jesus was actually given the wooden crossbeam to carry, rather than the entire cross, although this was a heavy burden for someone in his seriously weakened state. Jesus had just endured a dreadful scourging and must have lost a lot of blood. Wearing a crown of thorns fashioned for him by the mocking soldiers, Jesus was led through the narrow, stepped streets of Jerusalem. He was forced to carry the instrument of his death upon his back. But, as the Gospels record, Jesus fell down after taking only a few steps. The Roman guards, fearing that Jesus might die on the way, forced a bystander named Simon from Cyrene, to:

'shoulder the cross and carry it behind Jesus'
Luke 23:26.

Most of those who lined the route that Jesus took were horrified and stunned at what had happened:

> 'Large numbers of people followed him, who mourned and lamented for him.'
> Luke 23:27.

The nailing

The execution procession finally halted when it reached a small hill outside the city walls, aptly named *Golgotha*, a Hebrew word meaning *place of the skull*, or in Latin *Calvary*, (see *John* 19:17). Jesus was forced to lie on his back while nails were driven through his wrists (not, as was generally believed until recently, through his hands) to secure him to the crossbeam. Then, the crossbeam was lifted up and slotted onto an upright pole that stood permanently on the site. Once fixed in this position, Jesus' feet were nailed to the upright post and his body was probably tied to the cross with ropes to prevent it from tearing free. It is now understood that a cross would have had a small 'seat' fastened to the upright post on which the victim could rest his body weight. But, this was <u>not</u> an act of mercy, on the contrary, it had the effect of prolonging the person's life and thus his agony, as the person was constantly struggling to breathe.

The ordeal

Crucifixion was death by slow suffocation. A condemned person was hanged by his arms and this cut off the air supply to his lungs. In order to breathe, Jesus had to push down on the nails through his feet, which caused agonising pain. Even the strongest person could not survive this for long. Jesus endured this torture for six hours.

▲ Calvary by Mantegna (16th Century).

Annoyed at the way the Jewish elders had manipulated him, Pilate decided to have the last word and, deliberately seeking to insult them, he ordered that a placard be nailed on the upright beam above Jesus' head, reading:
Jesus of Nazareth, King of the Jews.

This infuriated the Sanhedrin delegates but Pilate refused to change it.

Jesus was left hanging between two thieves and the Roman guards gambled for his few possessions. All the while he could hear the insults of those who had plotted his death. They challenged Jesus to show that he was the Messiah by saving himself (see *Luke* 23:35). When faced with this nightmarish test, Jesus stayed true to his beliefs, saying of his enemies:

> *'Father, forgive them, for they know not what they are doing.'*
> Luke 23:34.

Another evangelist records the story that, before he died, Jesus looked down from the cross and . . .

> *'Seeing his mother and the disciple (John) standing near her, Jesus said to his mother, "Woman, this is your son." Then, to the disciple he said, "This is your mother". And from that moment the disciple made a place for her in his home.'*
> John 19:26–27.

Despite his agony, he still thought of the needs of others.

The death of Jesus

The Gospels of *Matthew* (27:45), *Mark* (15:33) and *Luke* (23:44) all assert that, about noon, an unusual darkness *'came over the whole land'* and lasted until about three o'clock that afternoon. Then, Jesus was offered a sponge soaked in vinegar diluted with water, which was held up to his lips with the aim of refreshing him and so keep him conscious for as long as possible. But, unexpectedly, after he had taken a drink, he said:

> *'"It is accomplished" and bowing his head, he gave up his spirit.'*
> John 19:30.

Luke, however, offers us a different version of Jesus' final statement, writing that:

> *'He said, "Father, into your hands I commend my spirit". With these words, he breathed his last.'*
> Luke 23:46.

Whether or not *Luke* accurately recorded Jesus' last words, this statement perfectly reflected the attitude in which Jesus had lived his entire life and to which he held true, even at the point of death. He put all his trust in the love of God the Father.

The importance of Jesus' death

According to *Mark* 15:38, *Matthew* 27:51 and *Luke* 23:45, when Jesus died *'the curtain of the Temple was torn in two'*. This most likely referred to the great curtain which hung over the entrance to the Holy of Holies, a place so sacred that only the high priest was allowed to enter it and then just once a year on the Day of Atonement. This may have happened as the evangelists said or it may have been a way of saying that through Jesus' death something of great importance had occurred:

- The curtain separated the people from the holiest part of the Temple where God was believed to dwell. <u>The sacrifice of Jesus had removed any barrier between God and human beings forever.</u> Before this only the High Priest was believed to have access to God. Through his death Jesus opened the way to God for everyone.
- The death of Jesus marked the end of the old covenant and the beginning of the new covenant.

QUESTIONS

(1) Describe the Roman method of crucifixion.
(2) Why did the Roman guards force Simon of Cyrene to help Jesus carry the heavy crossbeam?
(3) Read *Luke* 23:27. What was the reaction of most people who witnessed this event?
(4) What was the name of the place where Jesus was crucified?
(5) What was written on the placard Pilate ordered to be nailed on the upright beam of the cross above Jesus' head?
(6) Read *Luke* 23:34 and *John* 19:26–27. What do these statements reveal about Jesus?
(7) How long did Jesus suffer on the cross before he died? At what time on Good Friday is Jesus said to have died?
(8) What did the Jews believe about the Holy of Holies in the Temple?
(9) Read either *Mark* 15:38 or *Matthew* 22:51 or *Luke* 23:45. (a) What do they say happened at the same time that Jesus died on the cross? (b) What do Christian scholars believe is the meaning of this incident?

CHAPTER THIRTY

THE BURIAL OF JESUS

See *Mark* 15:42–47 *Luke* 23:50–56 *Matthew* 27:57–66 *John* 19:38–42

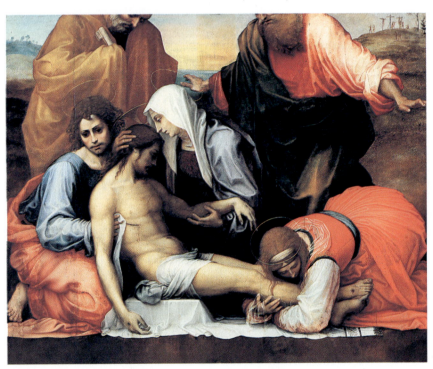

Della Porta's Deposition.

The removal of Jesus' body from the Cross

According to Jewish religious law, the body of a criminal could not be left displayed on a cross over the Sabbath. It had to be buried before nightfall (see *Deuteronomy* 21:22–23).

To ensure that Jesus and the two thieves crucified with him would be dead and buried before the Sabbath began that Friday evening at sundown, the Jewish leaders asked the Roman guards to break the prisoners' legs with a hammer, so that they could no longer hold themselves up to breathe. However, when the guards came to Jesus they realised that he was already dead. His death was due to a combination of massive blood loss, exhaustion and suffocation. But, to be absolutely sure that Jesus was dead, they pierced his side with a spear (see *John* 19:34).

The disciples had watched Jesus' last moments from a distance (see *Luke* 23:49). But they were not prepared to come forward to ask for permission to take down his body and bury it. They were too frightened. Instead, Joseph of Arimathea came forward and claimed Jesus' body for burial. Joseph was a member of the Sanhedrin who had supported Jesus and who now wished to distance himself from its actions.

Joseph had to get the permission of the Roman governor to have Jesus given a proper burial, as it was not usually allowed in the case of a crucified trouble-maker. (see *Luke* 24:50–52 and *John* 19:38).

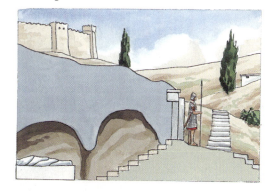

▲ The tomb of Jesus.

QUESTIONS

(1) Why did Jesus' body have to be taken down from the cross before sundown on Good Friday?

(2) What were the causes of Jesus' death?

(3) Read *John* 19:34. What did the Roman guards do to make certain that Jesus was dead?

(4) Who claimed Jesus' body for burial?

The burial

The burial itself was a rushed affair, because of the approaching Sabbath. It was decided that the women present would return on the Sunday morning, once the Sabbath was over, to embalm Jesus' corpse properly. For the time being it was:

> *'wrapped in a shroud and put in a tomb, which was hewn in stone in which no one had yet been buried'.*
> *Luke* 23:53.

The entrance to the tomb was sealed by rolling a large, heavy stone into place.

The closing up of the tomb was witnessed by Mary Magdelene and a group of Jesus' loyal women disciples, who had stayed with him when the Apostles had deserted him. Then they *'took note of where he was buried'*. *Mark* 15:47.

It is believed that the little tomb was in a garden, close to the city gates and *'near at hand'* (*John 19:42*) to where Jesus had been crucified.

Guarding the tomb

Caiaphas and the Sanhedrin no doubt hoped that the death of Jesus would finally put an end to the whole affair. But, they were apparently still worried that their troubles might not be entirely over yet. So the next morning, even though it was the Sabbath day, they sent a delegation to ask Pilate to provide a guard for Jesus' tomb. They explained their unusual request thus:

> *'Your excellency, we recall that this impostor said while he was still alive, "After three days, I shall rise again". Therefore, give the order to have the tomb kept secure until the third day, for fear his disciples will come and steal him away and tell the people, "He has risen from the dead". This last piece of fraud would be worse than what went before.'*
> Matthew 27:63–65

Pilate agreed to their request.

> *'So they went and made the tomb secure, putting seals on the stone and mounting a guard.'*
> Matthew 27:66

It is most unlikely that the Roman governor was worried about Jesus actually rising from the dead. His main concern was to ensure that there were no further disturbances during the Passover festival. Jerusalem was a city overflowing with people whom Pilate probably considered to be little more than an excitable rabble. If Jesus' followers were to steal the body from an unguarded tomb, who knew where all this might end? At the very least, it would reflect badly on Pilate if he had not taken the necessary precautions.

QUESTIONS

(1) Why did the women decide to return to the tomb on Sunday morning?

(2) Describe the tomb in which Jesus' body was placed?

(3) Read *Matthew 27:63–66*. What precautions did the Jewish authorities ask Pilate to take?

CHAPTER THIRTY-ONE

THE RESURRECTION

Introduction

Jesus died on the cross. He was buried in a tomb dug out of solid rock (see *Mark* 15:46). All his beautiful words about the Kingdom of God seemed to have been in vain. His story seemed to be over. Christians believe that it was only beginning.

The empty tomb

After the Jewish Sabbath had passed, a group of Jesus' women disciples went to the tomb early on the morning of what Christians call *Easter Sunday*. They brought with them spices to anoint Jesus' corpse. According to the earliest Gospel account (*Mark* 16:1) the women concerned were Mary Magdalene, Mary the mother of James and Salome (although *Luke* 24:10 identifies Joanna as the third woman).

In *John* 20:1, the evangelist simply notes that Mary Magdalene discovered that the stone covering the entrance had been rolled back and that she immediately ran to tell the disciples.

In contrast, the Synoptic Gospels offer more detailed accounts of the discovery of the empty tomb but differ in certain respects. See *Mark* 16:5–6 *Matthew* 28:2–6 and *Luke* 24:1–8.

When considering the historical value of these different versions of the same event, it is important to remember the following:
(1) The evangelists most likely used literary images such as a heavenly messenger(s) to emphasise the meaning and importance of this event.

▲ The empty tomb

▲ Piero della Francesca's The Resurrection of Christ (15th Century).

(2) The Synoptic Gospel accounts all agree on three essential points:
- A group of women went to the tomb.
- They found it empty.
- They heard an announcement that Jesus had risen from the dead.

N.B.
- It is important to remember that <u>no one actually saw Jesus rise from the dead</u>. The Gospels only deal with what happened afterwards.
- While all four Gospels record the resurrection of Jesus they differ in certain details. Then as now, no two people ever remember the same event in exactly the same way. However, when taken together they provide a powerful account of an extraordinary event.

QUESTIONS

(1) Who were the first of Jesus' followers to go to the tomb on Easter Sunday morning?

(2) Why did the authors of the Synoptic Gospels use such literary images as 'violent earthquakes' or 'angels' in the accounts describing the discovery of the empty tomb?

(3) On what points do the Synoptic Gospels agree concerning the discovery of the empty tomb?

(4) Did anyone actually witness Jesus rising from the dead on Easter Sunday morning?

The reaction of the Apostles

All four Gospels agree (*Mark* 16:7, *Matthew* 28:8, *Luke* 24:9 and *John* 20:2) that the women immediately went to where the disciples were hiding and reported what had happened. The Apostles reacted with total disbelief:

> 'When they heard that Jesus had risen . . . they did not believe it.'
> *Mark* 16:11

The Apostles were deeply upset and humiliated by the events of Good Friday. They believed that Jesus' mission had ended in total failure. He was dead. It was all over. When they heard what the women said about an empty tomb and a risen Jesus,

> 'Their words seemed to them like nonsense'. *Luke* 24:11.

However, Peter was unsure and, accompanied by John, he risked going to the tomb. There they discovered that it was indeed empty. Jesus' corpse was missing and the linen cloths in which it had been wrapped were lying on the floor of the tomb (see *John* 20:3–9).

The appearances of the risen Jesus

According to the *New Testament* a large number of people actually met and talked with Jesus after his death and burial. See 1 *Corinthians* 15:5–7, *Mark* 16:9–18, *Matthew* 28:9–10 and 16–20, *Luke* 24:13–49, *John* 20:10–31 and 21:1–14.

Drawing on these different accounts we can see that these separate appearances by Jesus included the following elements:

- Jesus unexpectedly revealed himself to them, usually greeting his astonished hosts with some reassuring words, such as *'Peace be with you'* (*John* 20:21).
- In each case all those present were initially shocked and frightened when they first saw the risen Jesus, a perfectly natural reaction in such an extraordinary set of circumstances.
- This shock and fear quickly faded away and was replaced by a great inner peace and joy when they realised that Jesus had risen.
- Jesus tells his followers to spread the news of his resurrection and told them to 'Go, therefore, make disciples of all nations' (*Matthew* 28:19).

▲ The risen Lord teaches his disciples.

These Gospel accounts make an extraordinary claim, but this claim is at the very heart of the Christian religion. As Paul later wrote:

> 'If Jesus has not been raised, then our preaching is useless and your believing in it is useless.'
> 1 *Corinthians* 15:14.

Christianity teaches that the resurrection of Jesus is a <u>historical fact</u> — Jesus actually died on Good Friday and rose from the dead on Easter Sunday.

The importance of the resurrection

It is a matter of profound importance for Christians that Jesus actually rose from the dead to a new and glorified life on Easter Sunday morning. Through his resurrection, Jesus shows us that:

- There is life after death.

Jesus died a cruel death but was raised up to new life through the power of God the Father. This same kind of resurrected life is offered to all those who faithfully struggle to follow Jesus in their everyday lives.

- Jesus is the promised Messiah.

The Old Testament prophecies that the Messiah would have to suffer, die and rise to new life on the third day were fulfilled in Jesus.
Jesus' resurrection is a sign that what he taught is true. God is our heavenly Father who is loving, just and forgiving.

- The power of good has triumphed over evil.

Through his resurrection Jesus offers hope to all humankind. He shows that death is not the end. His victory over death inspires people to follow his example and become his co-workers in building up the Kingdom of God. His rising gives confidence that what people do in this life has a real meaning and value, and that the good they do will be rewarded in the next life.

QUESTIONS

(1) What was the reaction of the eleven apostles when they heard the women's story of the empty tomb?

(2) How did Peter react to this news?

(3) According to 1 *Corinthians* 15:5–7, how many people witnessed the risen Jesus?

(4) Read *John* 20:19. What were Jesus' first words to his disciples? Why do you think he said this?

(5) What effect did Jesus' sudden appearance among them have on his disciples?

(6) Read *Matthew* 28:19. What command did Jesus give his disciples?

(7) State the three ways in which the resurrection of Jesus is of central importance for Christian belief.

CHAPTER THIRTY-TWO

QUESTIONS ABOUT THE RESURRECTION

Introduction

The claim that on Easter Sunday morning Jesus rose from the dead is a profoundly challenging one. Over the years since, many alternative explanations have been offered for the empty tomb.

[1] <u>Jesus did not die on Good Friday. He was merely unconscious when they took him down from the cross.</u>

Response:

- Both the Roman historian Tacitus and the Jewish historian Josephus accept that Jesus was condemned to death by Pontius Pilate and died on the cross.
- Roman executioners were very thorough. If the officer in charge failed to do his job properly then he risked being put to death himself.
- Jesus is said to have died after six hours on the cross — quite quickly for a crucified man but then he had also been the victim of a scourging. To make sure he was dead, the guards shoved a spear through his side.

[2] <u>Jesus' Jewish disciples were only too willing to believe in the idea of his resurrection and they would have had very little difficulty convincing their fellow Jews that he had risen.</u>

Response:

- People today are so familiar with the story of the resurrection that they do not realise how amazing it was for

Guercino's The Incredulity of St Thomas (17th Century).

both his disciples and those to whom they preached two thousand years ago. When the different disciples found the tomb empty or were told about it they were confused and did not believe he had risen. They did not expect something like Jesus' resurrection to happen. (see *Mark* 16:11, *Luke* 24:11, *John* 2:10–16 and 24–26).

The amazed disciples on finding the tomb empty.

- At that time there was considerable disagreement among the Jews about the whole idea of life after death. Basically there were two schools of thought:
  — the **Sadducees**, <u>did not</u> believe in life beyond the grave, stating that this life is all there is and when we die, that is the end of our existence.
  — the **Pharisees** and the greater majority of Jews <u>did</u> believe in life after death, but they thought two specific things about the resurrection:
  (i) it would only take place when the end of the world had come;
  (ii) it would be a <u>shared</u> experience, i.e. everybody who had lived a good life would be raised up to new life together.
- The Gospels make it quite clear how astonished and confused the disciples were by Jesus' appearances after his death (see *Matthew* 28:16–17, *Luke* 24:37–38, *John* 20:24–25). This was because the whole idea of a single individual person rising from the dead was an *unheard-of idea* among Jews at that time.
- If the disciples had deliberately set out to win over people to accept Jesus as the Messiah, then they chose a very strange way of doing it. The whole idea of Jesus' resurrection would have been very difficult for their fellow Jews to accept.

QUESTIONS

(1) What is the evidence to support the claim that Jesus died on the cross?

(2) What did (a) the Sadducees and (b) the Pharisees believe about life after death?

(3) Did the disciples expect that a single, individual person such as Jesus would rise from the dead within two days of his execution?

[3] <u>The disciples stole the body and invented the story of Jesus' resurrection.</u>

Response:
This accusation was first recorded in *Matthew* 28:13. Christian scholars believe it to be <u>untrue</u> for the following reasons:

- The Sanhedrin asked Pilate to put a guard on Jesus' tomb to prevent his body being removed by the disciples. It was an offence punishable by death for a Roman soldier to fall asleep on duty. The guards would have undoubtedly resisted any attempt to steal the corpse (see *Matthew* 27:63–66).

- Even if no guard had been present it is highly unlikely that the disciples would have done this. The execution of Jesus had shattered their confidence in him. They had lost hope and were not expecting to see Jesus again. They were afraid of being arrested and executed too. They did not leave their hiding place until they heard Mary Magdalene's news about the empty tomb. They would not have stolen the body. They were too frightened even to come forward and claim it for burial on Good Friday. They did not help to bury the body. They wanted to put the whole business behind them.

- If the Gospel writers wanted to make up a phoney story about Jesus rising from the dead, then they would never have identified Mary Magdalene, or the other women, as the first witnesses of the resurrection (see *Matthew* 28:9–10, *Mark* 16:9, *John* 20:10–18).

According to Jewish law at that time, a woman could <u>not</u> give evidence in court. Any writer who wanted to convince people that a hoax was genuine would never have chosen a woman as his primary witness, as her story would not usually have received a fair hearing in such a male-dominated society.

- Within days of Jesus' death, the disciples changed from shocked and humiliated people hiding in fear of their lives into brave and fearless preachers of Jesus' message. They openly preached that he was the

Messiah (or in Greek *'Christ'*) and that he was risen, even though they knew they risked death by doing so (see *Acts* 4:1–21).

In the years that followed, the disciples of Jesus journeyed far from their homeland spreading the news of his resurrection. All suffered great hardship and many paid for their devotion to Jesus with their lives (e.g. Peter was executed in Rome, Philip in Ethiopia and Thomas in India).

The disciples are highly unlikely to have gone to such great lengths if they had stolen the body. They would have lost interest in Jesus' message soon afterwards and their movement would probably have faded out under pressure of Roman persecution. It is highly unlikely that they would have endured poverty and persecution and even sacrificed their lives if it were all a lie.

QUESTIONS

(1) Read *Matthew* 28:13. Summarise the main points of this extract in your own words.

(2) According to *Matthew* 27:63–66, what did the Jewish leaders ask Pilate to do?

(3) If there had been no guard present at the tomb, is it likely that the disciples would have gone there and stolen the body?

(4) Why is it said that if the evangelists wanted to make up a phoney story then they would <u>not</u> have identified women as key witnesses?

(5) (a) Describe the change that came over the disciples in the days after Jesus' death? (b) What is believed to have <u>caused</u> this dramatic change?

[4] <u>What the disciples experienced after Jesus' death were ghostly apparitions.</u>

Response:
- Most Jews at that time believed in ghosts. At first glance, Jesus' various visits might seem to have been merely 'ghostly apparitions'. For example, the Gospels state that Jesus could suddenly appear in a locked room (*John* 20:19) and vanish at will (*Luke* 24:31).
- However, a more careful reading shows that the evangelists made it very clear that the risen Jesus was not some disembodied apparition, he was <u>not</u> a ghost.
- Firstly, Jesus appeared in bodily form to his disciples. For example, Jesus

was solid flesh and bone (see *Luke* 24:37–39), he had the marks of wounds on his body (see *John* 20:27) and ate food with his disciples (see *Luke* 24:41–43 and *Acts* 1:4). Whenever Jesus appeared he was physically, tangibly present.

- Secondly, although the accounts of the risen Jesus say that he could do things that are impossible for a human being to do, this does not necessarily mean that he was a ghost. The evangelists remarked throughout their accounts of Jesus' appearances that, though it was really Jesus people met, in some way he was <u>different</u> from the person they had known before. On some occasions they did not immediately recognise him (see *Mark* 16:12, *Luke* 24:15–16, *John* 20:14 and 21:4 and 12).

The evangelists found it very hard to explain that Jesus was alive but not in the same way as before his death. The disciples had seen Jesus bring Lazarus and Jairus' daughter back to life. They make it quite clear that Jesus had not been restored to his old earthly life as had Lazarus and Jairus' daughter.

Jesus was no longer limited by the physical laws of the universe that limit our human freedom of action. Jesus could walk through bolted doors and become tangible whenever he wanted. Through his resurrection Jesus' human body had been transformed or '<u>glorified</u>'. *Jesus was living a completely new kind of life.*

QUESTIONS

(1) Why might Jesus' visits with his disciples be thought of as 'ghostly apparitions'?

(2) What is the evidence in the Gospel accounts to support the belief that Jesus was <u>not</u> a ghost?

(3) Christians believe that, after his resurrection, '*Jesus was living a completely new kind of life*'. What do you think this means?

CHAPTER THIRTY-THREE

THE BIRTH OF CHRISTIANITY

Sources

Most of what is known about the first thirty years of the Christian community is to be found in the *Acts of the Apostles*. The author of *Acts* is the same person who wrote the Gospel of *Luke*. It takes up the story where the Gospel of *Luke* ends — with the ascension of Jesus into heaven (see *Luke* 24:50–53 and *Acts* 1:3–11).

The Ascension

Forty days after Easter Sunday, Jesus appeared to his disciples for the last time. His work on earth was finished. His disciples had finally come to realise that they were called to play a crucial role in establishing the reign of God in people's hearts. They drew enormous confidence from Jesus' promise that, although he would no longer be physically present among them, he would send them the Holy Spirit to give them the guidance and strength they would need for completing the work he had begun.

> *'After saying this, he was taken up to heaven as they watched him, and a cloud hid him from their sight.'*
> *Acts* 1:9.

When the evangelist wrote this he did not mean this to be taken literally, any more than when we say that someone moves up the school at the end of each academic year, we mean that he/she has gone up to the top floor of the building. *Taken up to heaven* means that Jesus was returning to a better or higher form of life with God the Father. *Luke* used these particular words in an effort to communicate an experience that was very difficult to put into words. The mention of the word *cloud* is to be expected here. The *Old Testament* writers often used the word cloud when they wanted to describe God's presence in some event.

Pentecost

Ten days after the Ascension the disciples gathered together to celebrate the Jewish harvest festival of Pentecost, from the Greek meaning the 50th day, because it was fifty days after Passover. They met in a room in Jerusalem. There they waited for the coming of the Holy Spirit as Jesus had promised:

> 'When Pentecost day came round, the apostles had all met in one room, when suddenly they heard what sounded like a powerful wind from heaven, the noise of which filled the entire house in which they were sitting: and something appeared to them that seemed like tongues of fire; they separated and came to rest on the head of each of them. They were all filled with the Holy Spirit.'
> Acts 2:1–4.

This experience of the Holy Spirit of God entering the lives of these disciples was so extraordinary that *Luke* found it very difficult to express it in words. When writing his account in *Acts*, he once again had to resort to using picture-language.

- The coming of the Holy Spirit upon the disciples was likened to the rushing of a '*powerful wind*' purifying their hearts.
- The courage and strength the disciples gained was like '*tongues of fire*' that lit up their hearts.

These images of wind and fire were frequently used in the *Old Testament* to convey the idea of God's power and goodness purifying and renewing those who opened their hearts and minds to his love. Not surprisingly, Pentecost Sunday became a popular date for christening new-born babies, because it was associated with the idea of new beginnings.

As a result of this Pentecost experience the disciples were fired up to begin fulfilling the great mission they had received from Jesus (see *Matthew* 28:16–20). They began openly preaching that Jesus was the Messiah, that he had risen and they began healing the sick in Jesus' name (see *Acts* 3:1–10).

Image of fire to symbolise courage and strength of the disciples.

QUESTIONS

(1) (a) In which *New Testament* book is the story of the first thirty years of the Christian community to be found? (b) Who wrote it?

(2) Why did Jesus promise to send the Holy Spirit to his disciples after his ascension into heaven?

(3) What do scholars believe the phrase *'taken up into heaven'* means?

(4) What did *Old Testament* Jewish writers use the word *cloud* to indicate?

(5) Why did the author of *Acts* use picture-language in his account of the Holy Spirit descending on the disciples at Pentecost?

(6) What did *Old Testament* writers use the images of *wind* and *fire* to say about God?

(7) What effect did this Pentecost experience have on the disciples?

Confrontation

The Sadducees in particular became troubled by the disciples' references to Jesus' resurrection. The chief priests had Peter and John arrested on two occasions in an effort to intimidate them. The disciples could not be persuaded to stop preaching and healing.

On the second occasion, the rabbi Gamaliel spoke to the assembled Sanhedrin members.

> 'In the present case I advise you: Leave these men alone! Let them go! For if their purpose or activity is of human origin, it will fail. But if it is from God, you will not be able to stop these men; you will only find yourselves fighting against God.'
> Acts 5:38–39.

The Sanhedrin accepted this advice. The two Apostles were flogged and again banned from preaching about Jesus. It is quite likely that Gamaliel's advice saved the Apostles' lives. But Jesus' disciples would not stay silent. They continued to preach and to heal and their numbers grew steadily.

Rabbi Gamaliel, pleading for the release of Peter and John.

The Gospel spreads

By the end of the first century A.D. there were Christian communities in Palestine, Asia Minor, North Africa, Greece and Italy. The Christian message probably first spread from Palestine through the network of Jewish communities that existed in other parts of the empire. These Jews living outside Palestine were known as the '*Diaspora*' (from the Greek word meaning 'dispersion'). This transmission of the Gospel message throughout the empire was greatly assisted by the excellent road network which Rome had built to ensure the safe travel and swift communication necessary for the effective government of such a vast territory.

QUESTIONS

(1) How did the Sadducees react to the preaching and healing by the Apostles?

(2) Read *Acts* 5:38–39 again. Write out Gamaliel's advice in your own words.

(3) What effect did Gamaliel's advice have on the Sanhedrin?

(4) What was the *Diaspora*?

(5) How did the Christian message quickly spread from Palestine throughout the Roman empire?

CHAPTER THIRTY-FOUR

THE EXPANSION OF CHRISTIANITY

The death of Stephen

As more and more Jews began to ask for baptism and join the disciples, this provoked fierce discussion among the Jews in Jerusalem. Tensions began to rise. The Temple authorities acted to stop what they considered to be a plot to destroy the Law of Moses and the Temple (see *Acts* 6:11 and 13–14).

A young disciple named Stephen was put on trial for blasphemy. He bravely defended himself before the Sanhedrin (see *Acts* 7:1–53). However, Stephen's trial ended in a riot and he was stoned to death by an angry mob (*Acts* 7:54–60).

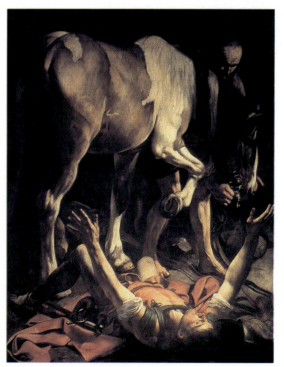

The Conversion of Paul on the road to Damascus by Carivaggio.

Antioch

After this many *Christians* (meaning: followers of Christ, from the Greek word for Messiah — *Christos*) decided to leave Jerusalem. Many Christians went to Alexandria in Egypt, Antioch in Asia Minor and Damascus in Syria. There they preached the Gospel to gentiles, many of whom asked to be baptised. For the first time in history Jews and gentiles gathered together to worship God. The Jesus they believed in was not just the Messiah of the Jews but *the Christ of all humankind.*

Paul

Though the twelve apostles (see *Acts* 1:13 and 26) played a vital role in the early success of Christianity, most scholars agree that the most outstanding Christian missionary of the first century A.D. was *Paul* (or in Hebrew *Saul*) of Tarsus. Before he became a Christian, Paul had been a devout Pharisee who had persecuted the Christians in Jerusalem.

While journeying to Damascus in Syria, where he intended to persecute the Christians there, Paul had an extraordinary and sudden conversion to Christianity (see *Acts* 9:1–19). Instead of persecuting the Christians, Paul joined them (see *Acts* 9:20–31).

Not surprisingly, the Jewish authorities decided to arrest Paul on a charge of *heresy* (i.e. spreading false ideas about God). Paul escaped and set out on the first of three great missionary journeys.

Paul was uniquely well-equipped to spread the Christian religion. Though Jewish by religion, he was a Roman citizen by birth. He spoke Aramaic, Greek, Hebrew and Latin, and so could communicate with a wide variety of people, both Jews and gentiles.

Paul travelled tirelessly throughout the eastern Mediterranean area, spreading the Christian message, baptising people and setting up communities in every town and city he visited. His *epistles*, i.e. letters written offering advice to these new Christian communities, testify to his wide-reaching influence.

▲ St Paul teaching in Athens.

QUESTIONS

(1) Why was Stephen put on trial by the Sanhedrin?

(2) (a) Where did many Christians go after Stephen's death? (b) How did this help to spread the Christian message?

(3) What is an *epistle*?

(4) What is *heresy*?

(5) Write a brief essay on the important role played by Paul in the spread of Christianity.

Moment of decision

A problem soon arose for the new Christian converts who had not been Jews beforehand. Did they need to become Jews first before they could become Christians? Did they have to be circumcised <u>before</u> they were baptised?

A general council of Christian leaders, the first of its kind, was held in Jerusalem in A.D. 49 to answer these questions. After a long debate, Paul won the support of Peter and the majority of those present to his solution. Peter, as leader of the Christian community, declared that new converts did not have to become Jews first before becoming Christians. Repentance for one's sins and baptism were all that one needed to become a member of the Christian community. As Paul wrote:

> 'All baptised in Christ, you have all clothed yourselves in Christ, and there are no more distinctions between Jew and Greek, slave and free, male and female, but all of you are one in Christ Jesus.'
> Galatians 3:27–28.

With the council of Jerusalem's decision to sever the Christian communities' links with Judaism, Christianity became a clearly separate world religion. It sought to draw in people of all different races and become a *Universal* or *Catholic* faith. Within a few years, Christian missionaries were spreading Jesus' message in Ethiopia, Spain, Northern India and China.

Worship

Until the Emperor Constantine granted freedom of worship to Christians in the Edict of Milan in A.D. 313, Christians had to worship in secret for fear of persecution. As a result, the earliest known <u>church</u>, (i.e. building specifically designed for Christian worship) dates from the fourth century A.D. Until then, Christians met in a room in the private house of a believer.

As a mark of their separation from Judaism, Christians stopped observing the Sabbath on Saturday and moved it to Sunday, the day of Jesus' resurrection. The format of the <u>Mass</u> was established very early:

- The faithful sang hymns
- Listened to readings from the sacred scriptures and
- Took part in a <u>eucharist</u>, i.e. a communal meal modelled on the Last Supper, where bread and wine were offered in thanksgiving for and remembrance of the life, death and resurrection of Jesus.

As Christianity's message spread and its ranks swelled with new members, it quickly developed new forms of organisation:

- <u>Presbyters</u> (i.e. priests) were selected to conduct religious services such as baptism and eucharist and to give religious instruction to new-comers.
- The chief priest in each area (called a <u>diocese</u>) was known as the <u>bishop</u>, from the Greek *'Episkopos'* meaning 'overseer' or 'guardian'.

These clergymen did not, however, wear any distinctive vestments until the fourth century A.D. The altar they used was usually just a simple wooden table in a room. This was necessary because, if the Roman authorities should raid the house, all they would apparently find would be a group of friends sharing a simple meal of bread and wine.

Persecution

It was the sudden and widespread growth of Christianity throughout the empire that first brought it to the attention of the Roman authorities. By the middle of the first century A.D., they viewed Christians with growing suspicion for several reasons:

- The Romans were <u>polytheists</u> (i.e. believed in many gods). They were tolerant of the religious beliefs of their conquered subjects so long as they worshipped one extra god — <u>the emperor</u> — as a guarantee of their loyalty. Only one group — the Jews — had been excused from doing this, in gratitude for Herod the Great once helping Julius Caesar. This exemption had been granted to the Christians too, until the Romans realised that the Christians were no longer Jews but a new, separate religion. When Christians refused to worship a pagan god, particularly the emperor, the Romans considered them disloyal.
- Christians refused to attend the popular, bloodthirsty games and encouraged others to boycott them.
- The Roman historian Tacitus mentions how ugly rumours that Christians were cannibals began to circulate, causing them to be <u>'hated for their abominations'</u>.

[The Annals]

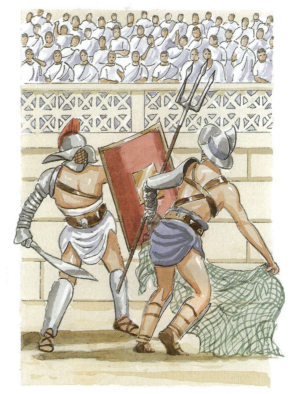

Colosseum in Nero's time.

All About Faith

▲ Rome burning.

When a terrible fire destroyed much of the city of Rome in A.D. 64, the Emperor Nero, whom many suspected as having caused the fire, claimed that the Christians were responsible instead. Cleverly exploiting popular opinion, Nero launched a vicious persecution of the Christians.

The Roman mob was treated to a series of cruel public spectacles in which thousands of Christians were put to death in the arena, or crucified and set alight to provide illumination for one of Nero's outdoor banquets. According to Christian tradition, both Peter and Paul were put to death during this persecution.

Despite this horrific episode and other terrible periods of repression over succeeding centuries, the Christian faith did not die out as the Roman authorities had expected. On the contrary, it continued to thrive and survived many other periods of uncertainty and persecution. Today it is the largest religion on earth with one in three human beings declaring themselves followers of Jesus Christ.

QUESTIONS

(1) What was the problem facing Christians who had not been Jews before their conversion?

(2) What was decided at the Council of Jerusalem?

(3) What does the word *catholic* mean?

(4) Give one example of how the early Christians marked their separation from Judaism.

(5) Explain the origin and meaning of the title *bishop*.

(6) Imagine you are a Christian living in Rome during the reign of the emperor Nero. Explain why the Roman authorities are persecuting Christians.

CHAPTER THIRTY-FIVE

THE TITLES OF JESUS

Before the resurrection

From the beginning of Jesus' public ministry, people were asking *'who is this?'* (*Mark* 1:27). Jesus seems to have been reluctant at first to encourage speculation about his identity (see *Mark* 3:12). He probably resisted being publicly identified as the Messiah to avoid raising popular expectations that he was going to lead a revolt against Roman rule (see *John* 6:15).

But Jesus could not stop people from wondering about him. Eventually he asked his disciples *'Who do you say I am?'* (*Matthew* 16:14). It was Peter who realised that Jesus was the Messiah.

▲ Icon of Jesus.

After the resurrection

After the disciples met the risen Jesus they realised that, while he was the promised Messiah/Christ, he was also much more. Jesus was an utterly unique person. They found this very hard to express in words.

In the *New Testament*, the early Christian writers used a number of titles to express their insights into Jesus' true identity:

- The Son of Man
- The Lord
- The Son of God.

The Son of Man

In Hebrew the phrase *son of man* simply means *human being*. This is the only specific title that Jesus is recorded as having directly applied to himself. At first glance, Jesus seems to have used this title merely as a way of referring to himself, as a person today might say <u>I</u> or <u>me</u>.

But on closer inspection we can see that he meant something more. When questioned by the high priest (see *Mark* 16:61–62) Jesus quoted from the *Old Testament* book of *Daniel*: in it the title *the Son of Man* referred to the <u>Messiah</u>.

Also Jesus used the title *the Son of Man* when he revealed that:

- He had the power to forgive sins,
- He was Lord of the Sabbath,
- He would suffer and die
- He will return again at the end of time for the final judgment of the human race.

Jesus claimed that he, <u>the Son of Man, was able to do things that were proper only for God to do</u>. This raised huge issues about the identity of Jesus that the early Christians took many years to work out.

The Lord

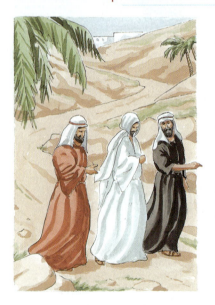

▲ Jesus with two disciples on the road to Emmaus.

The Jewish people believed that God's name was *Yahweh*. However, they considered God's name to be so holy that it should never be either spoken or written. Instead, they substituted the title *Lord* for God's name. The Gospels show that before his death and resurrection, Jesus himself used this title when speaking to or about God, whom he called <u>his Father</u>.

However, after his resurrection the first Christians, who were still loyal Jews worshipping at the Temple, were calling Jesus *the Lord* (see *Acts* 2:36). They believed that Jesus had revealed that he actually possessed authority and power that belong only to God (see *John* 20:28).

By calling Jesus *the Lord* or *our Lord*, they were saying that he was somehow <u>united with God</u> and they claimed a <u>divine</u> identity for Jesus.

The Son of God

It was not unheard of for first century Jews to refer to an exceptionally good person as '*a son of God*'. As the early Christians reflected on the words and actions of Jesus they gradually came to place greater emphasis on his references to God as <u>his</u> Father (see *Matthew* 11:25–27 and *Mark* 12:1–12). By the time the fourth Gospel — *John* — came to be written, Christians had come to better appreciate the <u>uniquely close</u> relationship Jesus had with God.

When the early Christians had referred to Jesus as *the Son of Man* and *the Lord*, they were pointing to Jesus being far more than an exceptionally good person. They realised that Jesus' entire life revealed a total one-ness with God in all he said and did. So much so that Jesus shared in God's very nature. They began to refer to Jesus as '*the Son of God*'. (see *John* 1:18, 3:16, 10:36 and 20:31).

QUESTIONS

(1) Why was Jesus reluctant to encourage speculation about his identity?

(2) Who was the first disciple to identify Jesus as the Messiah?

(3) To whom did the title '*the Son of Man*' refer in the Book of *Daniel*?

(4) When Jesus used the title '*the Son of Man*' what did he reveal about himself?

(5) To whom was the title '*the Lord*' addressed in the *Old Testament*? Why was it used?

(6) When did Christians begin to apply this title to Jesus?

(7) Read *John* 20:28. Why does Thomas use this title when addressing the risen Jesus?

(8) By the time the fourth Gospel — *John* — came to be written, Christians had begun referring to Jesus by what title?

(9) Why had they come to realise this about Jesus?

Concluding remarks

The evangelists make it quite clear that Jesus was a real human being who got hungry, thirsty and tired. He experienced the full range of human emotions, including joy and sorrow. He bled and died on the cross. But after his resurrection, the disciples *worshipped Jesus* (see *Matthew* 28:17, and *Luke* 24:52). Each of them came to acknowledge Jesus as '*my Lord and my God*' (*John* 20:28).

As we have seen, the evangelists struggled to find words to express the identity of Jesus. They gave him various titles, which we have examined. Finally they concluded that in Jesus Christ — God became a human being. This is called the Christian doctrine (i.e. teaching) of *the Incarnation*.

This was an extraordinary conclusion for Jesus' early followers to reach. The first Christians had been devout Jews who believed in one God. As Christians they still believed in one God. But as we shall see later, their whole idea of God was transformed and expanded by their encounter with and faith in Jesus Christ.

Photo Acknowledgments

Photographs are reproduced by permission of the following:

E.T. Archive, p.39, p.43, p.47, p.48, p.103, p.127;

SCALA, p.31, p.32, p.124, p.131;

Sonia Halliday Photographs, p.25, p.38, p.52, p.53, p.55, p.58, p.65, p.66, p.70, p.78, p.81, p.83, p.87, p.97, p.102, p.106, p.115, p.116, p.120;

Juliette Soester, AMPA, p.25;

The John Rylands University Library, p.15;

The Bridgeman Art Library, p.10, p.15, p.57, p.68, p.102, p.121, p.140;

Robert Harding, p.1, p.57, p.80.